Foreword

by Johnny Vaughan

I'd like to have started this by telling you, in the time honoured tradition of all book introductions, that the author has an enthusiasm for his subject that is so genuine, warm and infectious that it 'just can't help rubbing off on you'. In the case of Kevin Horkin though, this would be woefully understating his enthusiasm for our four legged friends. The man is obsessed.

Luckily, for the last three years my wife and I have benefited from Kev's encyclopaedic knowledge of dogs when he's been our guide around Crufts. He can not only identify nearly all of the 150 assorted breeds being shown, but he can generally tell you what dog any given show goer has at home just by looking at them. And that's Kevin's passion: not just dogs, not just owners, but the 'thing' that dogs and owners share together. Which is, essentially, what this book is all about. That 'thing'. Some use the word 'relationship' to describe this bond, but for me it comes with too much human baggage. Relationships with human's have ups and downs, good days/weeks/years and bad ones, and are fraught with complexities. Not so the 'thing' you have with your dog. If you've been in a 'relationship' with a human for a few years and you come home from work, they don't leap about the kitchen, jump on you, bark, and scratch on the lavatory door, if you've a bursting bladder on arrival and haven't had time to greet them properly. Unless of course you're going out with a Viagra tester. And if my wife came down in the morning and found me crashed out on the kitchen floor with a big pool of urine in front of me she'd hardly say, in a sympathetic, coo-chee-coo voice. "Did you get caught short in the night", as she did when our Bulldog was old enough to know better and still having 'accidents' in the night. She'd call up alcoholics anonymous after making it perfectly clear that I was in the doghouse for the foreseeable future. (Ironically a place we rarely send dogs.)

On the subject of dogs, mine is a year old Bulldog who's just learning to slobber. He sleeps about 17 hours a day, but however crashed out he is, and his snoring sounds like someone sawing through an oaktree, he is by your side as soon as there's even the most inaudible rustle of a food wrapper. Like some sleek, food seeking missile.

He barks when there's danger, squirrels, cats or hoover's around, he regularly can't make it back from walks, (especially if he's been playing with this pack of local Labradors in the park and he forgets that he's not a run-all-day gun dog), and he loves sniffing pensioners – even more so when they've been drinking and are all 'friendly'.

Despite having to clean up his doings every day, and mop out his facial folds with baby wet ones; I'm so glad Kevin recommended Bulldog ownership so strongly to me when I was dog window shopping. He said they'd fit in perfectly with my lifestyle and sent me a book as soon as he heard I'd bought a puppy. Interestingly, when I opened it up the first sentence read, "The Bulldog is the ultimate lazy-man's dog", which might say a bit about the way he see's my 'lifestyle', but it also says quite a lot about his own since he owns at least 6 Bulldogs himself.

Anyway, Kevin once said to me that it doesn't matter what the judges at Cruft's think – you always go home with the best dog, and in some ways, I think it's the same with this book: You'll see, and learn about, Star Dogs, but you know the real Star Dog is the one, I hope, is snoring away at your feet while you're reading

Best wishes

Johnny

Johnny Vaughan

P.S. Do you think if you managed to get to the p.a. system at the Birmingham NEC during Crufts and shouted "WALKIES!" you'd get arrested

*Kevin's other books in the series –
'Pets and Personalities on Coronation Street' in association with Granada TV. And 'Pets and Personalities'.*

*The fourth book in the series will be
Hollywood Star Dogs.*

Acknowledgements

Grateful thanks are due to the following for their assistance -

Bill King (Pedigree Masterfoods)

Jane Howard (Editor),

Vince Hogan and the 'Our Dogs' team

Jonathan Rimmer, Essential Design (design and artwork)

Wendy and Roy

Credits for photography -

Harold Holborn

Marc Henrie

'Mad About Dogs'

Mike Dancer

Ken Lennox (News of the World)

The Sun

Daily Mail

Granada TV

G.M.T.V.

Capital

BBC TV

Dedication -

I would like to dedicate this book to all the personalities and their wonderful canine companions
who have contributed their time and their personal and individual stories
for the benefit of The Pet Role Trust.

And Finally...

... a special acknowledgement to a very dear friend, 'Garbray Bric-a-brac —
more affectionately known as 'Miss Blanche'.

Introduction

by Roy Barraclough

Rovers of many kinds have played varying roles in my life - there was that pub of course, Alec was one of the greatest rovers of all time and then there's my love of dogs ... all dogs but most especially Westies.

For many years I had a Westie called Whiskey who was a loyal and devoted friend. When I was doing television work like 'Coronation Street' some dear friends looked after her but she often came with me to theatres and would sit for hours in the dressing room - no trouble at all. She did get the acting bug though, she appeared in a couple of episodes of the 'Street' being walked by an 'extra' - she would always act the part and studiously ignore me as Alec! She also joined me on stage in pantomimes (she had her own nurses outfit once!) and she appeared with Les Dawson and me in summer season at Blackpool. Her finest moment though was as the last (and most important) guest on my 'This is Your Life' tribute.

Sadly, Whiskey passed away some years ago and I've never replaced her - I travel a lot more these days and there's no one around to look after a dog. Not long after Whiskey died I was asked to become a patron of the 'Manchester Home For Lost Dogs' who do wonderful work throughout the North West and actually take in more dogs than the more famous Battersea - over 10,000 a year. In the past couple of years the work of the Home has expanded and they now have two sites, a hospital, neutering centre and a pet cemetery but they rely solely on donations to continue their good work. Sadly, the need for their expansion reveals the increase in cruelty cases and abandonment particularly of older dogs. However, if through lending my support they can achieve a higher profile then at least I'm able to pay back some of the love Whiskey gave me over all our years together.

It is very easy as dog lovers to forget the need to support rescue homes but it is up to us to do everything we can to pay back that love.

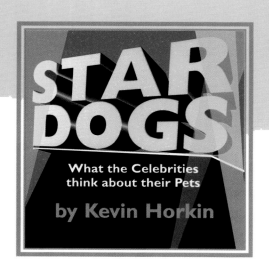

© Kevin Horkin of The Pet Role Trust

Published in association with

The Our Dogs Publishing Company Limited (Est. 1895)
5 Oxford Road Station Approach, Manchester M60 1SX
Telephone 0161 236 2660 Fax 0161 236 5534
www.ourdogs.co.uk

First Published 2000
The Our Dogs Publishing Company Limited
ISBN 0 903034 17 4

Contents

Pet Role Album

Kevin has been called upon to advise for programmes such as World in Action and Newsnight on many of the serious topical dog issues of the day, for example, the ending of quarantine and new passports for pets, and the dangerous dogs legislation.

On top of that, Kevin's agency - Pet Role - has supplied a vast number of the four-legged, feathered and furry stars for the best of British entertainment. He has been a regular contributor and pet consultant to This Morning and Coronation Street.

Pet Role's animal actors have starred in ITV's **Touch of Frost**, **The Sooty and Sweep Show**, **Pat Phoenix Love Story**, and **You've Been Framed**. Plus for the BBC, **Common as Muck**, **City Central** and **Blue Peter**.

Pet Role is asked to provide some really amazing animal stars.

Usually it's domestic pets, such as cats and dogs, but there are more exotic assignments too. One that sticks in Kevin's mind has been finding a Black Panther for a diamond commercial, and a reindeer for a Christmas variety show.

Kevin's house is like a retirement home for animal actors – he has Jack Duckworth's pigeons, Natalie's cat Tiger, even Teresa the Turkey from Coronation Street - the only turkey that looks forward to Christmas and one of the oldest in Britain. She has survived five Christmases! Richard and Judy's favourite is Snowy the Donkey, a regular on the Christmas week shows, who lives nearby.

The main aim throughout all Kevin's animal-related work is to promote responsible pet ownership.

Kriss Akabusi needs no introduction, that boom of a laugh alone is known the world over! He is absolutely so much a part of our sporting scene, and making inroads with commentating, that his face is as well known as our own in the mirror. He shares his life with wife Monika, his two delightful daughters Ashanti and Ahakira, and Dillinger the Doberman.

Kriss's early life was spent in Nigeria. He was born in Britain in 1958 but the whole family returned to Nigeria in 1960. But his mother pretty soon realised that there weren't the opportunities for her to both support the family and work as a nurse in her native Nigeria, so she left the children in the care

Kriss Akabusi

of her family and returned to Britain. Kriss's father was also in Britain studying international law and politics. The irony was that his parents didn't meet until they came to Britain in 1955 but discovered that they came from neighbouring villages back in Nigeria!

The Biafran war upset the plans of the family and Kriss and his younger brothers found themselves in a children's' home. It wasn't unhappy but the life-changing bonus was that the home had two Border Collies. He loved those two dogs and resolved that he would have dogs one day himself. It was a long time but he got there in the end.

His early career in the army is instructive. At 16 Kriss joined the British Army, though even at 22 in the PT corps he had no burning desire to become an athlete. "When I was 19 I started training because that's what the Sergeant Major told me to do and this was the Army so we did it.

"I wanted to be an army champion but I never thought further than that. Then I thought it might be good to be inter-service champion but I'd never even been to an AAA (Amateur Athletics Association) meeting. My friend in the army coaxed me into the championships but I wanted to be a big fish in a small pond. They called me Akabusi the Flyer!" So Kriss went on to the National Championship in 1983 and the world at large started to notice the Flyer. He was asked to compete in Russia for Great Britain and was innocent enough to worry whether his Sergeant Major would let him have time off!

"When I put on the British vest I grew to ten feet tall. I was so proud". He returned to civvy street in Germany and Dillinger the first joined the family.

Why Dobermans? "I was completely taken by a film called the Doberman gang a

strong powerful and fast dog that was part of a bank robbing outfit and knew the dog for me was the Doberman. Dillinger was one of the gang, not as most people think, 'public enemy number one'. The first Dillinger had to be left in Germany because of the quarantine laws and sadly he died very young. Dillinger the second who shares Kriss's birthday - 28 November - lives with

the family on the South Coast, running in and out of the sea, accompanying Kriss on training runs, and generally putting on a pretty good act that he is enjoying himself.

His happiest day? "The day the Prime Minister's office phoned to ask if I would accept an MBE if offered. I thought it was a wind-up, just out of the blue. Can you imagine turning it down?"

With a wonderful singing voice, plenty of cheeky-chappie charm and good looks, Michael Ball has them crying in the aisles at the musicals that are the backbone of the current London West End. He's a showman extraordinaire. He has been the darling of Andrew Lloyd Webber's set for about 10 years now and his face and voice have graced the biggest scene-stealing numbers to come out of such shows as 'Phantom of the Opera', 'Aspects of Love' and 'Les Miserables'.

He may not have been around long but he has certainly left a lasting impression! He started out as an actor who sang and as we know changed track midway to be a singer who can act! There are many more surprises in store.

You'd be quite surprised to discover the dog that inhabits Michael Ball's heart. You might expect something like an elegant Doberman, a Setter or a long-legged Wolfhound – but no. It's a Tibetan Terrier and he has become something of an authority on the breed. "My girlfriend Cathy had a Tibetan Terrier when we first got together. He was called Oscar

Michael Ball

and was 16 years old, already going blind and deaf. Sadly he developed cancer and they felt the kindest thing was to have him put to sleep. We both stayed with him while he had the injection. It was all such a trauma. But now we have Yogi – also a Tibetan Terrier – who is like a surrogate child."

"Tibetan Terriers are quite a rare dog and there are two types, the Luvil and the Langley. Luvil are the bigger type and slightly more sensible. Yogi is a Langley and they tend to be completely neurotic, in fact they say they become exactly like their owners. Originally they were used by Tibetan farmers for herding. They are a one-man dog, and can be very jealous of their owner. If Cath and I have a cuddle he jumps between us, barking and going mental!"

Michael Ball was brought up in South Africa but spent his school life here in Britain. When the family returned they had to leave behind a handsome young Labrador called Ben, "Who is still going strong." Quarantine laws are archaic. When I was doing Aspects of Love the leading lady was an American, Ann Crumb, and her two rescue dogs were in quarantine. It was heartbreaking for her and for them. It's like a prison only they don't know why they are there. They had all their shots against Rabies and as long as they have their injection I don't see a problem with any of it.

Would he consider a rescue dog? "We had a rescue Bull Mastiff for a while, from Battersea Dogs Home. She was such a wonderful old lady. Ella was her name and she had lived with two other Bull Mastiffs in a flat. She was the survivor of a dreadful experience but we enjoyed nursing her back to full health."

Does Michael have views on how best to choose a dog? "I went to Battersea but to be honest I found it too upsetting. I couldn't stay there. I think dogs should come from a reputable kennel if you want a good pedigree or from rescue homes. You've got to be prepared to make sacrifices for them, you can't leave them on their own, you've got make time to exercise them, to show them affection and to show them love. They're like humans, they need to be shown that they are loved and it's like having a child that doesn't grow up."

What have you learnt from pets and from life. "From my pets I have learnt about love and forgiveness, from life I have learnt that nothing is for certain!"

Cilla Black

Everyone knows Cilla, she's had a lorra lorra luck, but built on a lorra lorra talent. Having started in the 60s at the time when the Mersey Beat provided the pulse for pop, she has carved out her place as a Great British institution. The current show, prime time Saturday night, "Blind Date" has people from all walks of life intrigued and inspired. Her private life is as private as it can be, but her love of animals has grown up with her and she obviously considers animals of all sorts an important addition to family life. So which dogs share her life at the moment?

"I've got Denver, a Briard and we've got Coffee who's a mongrel. We've had so many dogs. I got Denver as a puppy, I wanted to call him Dillon, but we've always kept the names that they've come with. We thought that it was time now we've got over our grief for Panda – so let's get another dog, and then I thought, I think this dog needs a little friend. So, I was reading the Daily Mail one day and I read that three dogs, Coffee, Tea and Sugar were abandoned in a cardboard box outside Sainsbury's and I thought, 'Oh dear', and I actually cut the photograph out of the paper and put it down on the kitchen floor and I said to Denver, 'Which one shall we try and go for?' A big wet nose landed on Coffee, and I was so thrilled because apparently the phone had never stopped ringing for these dogs and we got her anyway. Obviously she's the boss, she's about 12 inches long and tiny, and the Briard's like about nine stone!" But she evidently feels lost without a dog in her life, preferably two.

Cilla has already hinted that dogs and animals of all sorts have been part of her life for many years. So, where did it all start, what kind of pets did she have as a child?

Cilla reveals that she had the usual assortment of cats, budgies and dogs. But the favourite was the dog. "You shouldn't really have favourites with animals, but I have to say the dog – our Lassie. I remember, my dad, he used to work on the docks, my mother was a real sucker for little puppies and he'd gone to the pub for a drink and someone had brought this pup in – obviously a crossbreed – between a Collie and a God knows what other dog, and she did look like a Lassie dog and she lived for an awfully long time – she was nearly 14 when she died."

Cilla's voice has not lost any of the broad Liverpool, and she rattles off her memories at her usual breakneck speed with a tone that's cross between a laugh and a song.

She obviously feels that pets are very important to families with children growing up, that children learn their early relationships from living with a pet, whether it's a dog, cat, fish or fowl.

"You have to have pets, it's very important for children. All my boys, I've got three sons –they've always had dogs and rabbits. It's very, very important – I think they make a nice companion."

Apart from Coffee and Denver, what pets does she have now?

"I have an aviary with 30 budgies and cockatiels, eight parakeets as well as two dogs. We've always had a Briard, and in fact I got my very first Briard when I was watching Blue Peter on the telly – it was the first Briard pup to be born and bred in Britain. First of all we got our Sophie, and then we were up in Blackpool doing the summer season and – you see I think dogs should always have a mate – whether it be a cat or another dog – and both of us just felt we'd like to get a mate for our Sophie so we rang the same lady and we got Ada, who was Sophie's sister, yes Ada. And I have to say the names should have been the opposite way round because Ada looks more like a Sophie and Sophie looks like the runt of the litter but she was fabulous."

Cilla rattles through another breathless list of the dogs she has owned in her life. Sophie and Ada are both dead now. "But I did breed from both of them and I had two dogs from each litter. One litter was called after Shakespearean characters and the other after districts in Liverpool. So I kept Dingle from Sophie's litter and Theo. I married my Bobby in 1969, you can imagine we got through a lot of dogs in our married life. The Briard's always been my favourite. The only time we didn't get a Briard was when we lost Theo and Dingle, and we were so upset for a while. But then as unluck would have it, we were burgled so we decided to get Panda, a Doberman. He was gorgeous but quite frightening. Panda fell in love with our new Briard, Hazel, a blonde Briard.

"We had always wanted a blonde Briard, because all the other Briards were black, so we got this eight month old dog, Hazel, she was gorgeous. We took her to the vet, the normal thing that you do and the vet said that she

should have been put to sleep because of the hip thing. The breeder said he would take her back, but she'd been with us for a week and we loved her, so we couldn't just send her back. She was fabulous, so good natured and loving."

Cilla is obviously barmy about Briards, but what breed of dog would she choose if Briards were off-limits?

"The thing is that if you like animals and you like dogs – I tend not to think about their breed but their personalities. When we went to buy Denver, he chose us. He was the one that left his litter and came over to us, so we said we'll have that puppy.

"There are lots of breeds, all these animal shows that are on the telly – really you'd have to put me in

handcuffs and tie my hands down, because I'm ready to reach for the phone – you know programmes like 'Give this dog a home' well, really, any animal. These animals have to be taken care of and the thing is at Christmas time, not that I would want to go away at Christmas time, but we could never ever go away at Christmas because of the dogs, so we wouldn't go away unless there was somebody to look after them."

Cilla is obviously mad about dogs, emphasising that to have a dog is quite a commitment, and she touches on responsible pet ownership. When asked if she could only say one thing from having owned animals about how to be a responsible pet owner, "You can't say more than a pet is more than just for Christmas, it's an extension of your family – and what you wouldn't do to your children certainly don't do to your animals."

There's the old adage about showbiz types not working with animals and children. Has she ever worked with animals professionally?

"I did a long time ago a Disney special, on a bank holiday at Blackpool. It was wonderful, but I had to sit next to a monkey…" She can remember all too clearly what happened, the monkey was not a professional! "He forgot all his lines!"

"We have used quite a few animals on Surprise Surprise. I remember a woman who really would have loved to hold a baby lamb – of course you can't train baby lambs – she was wonderful and the lamb, I'd loved to have had her – it was shining that night, Lady Luck, because as I stroked the lamb it baaaed back at me – you can't buy that."

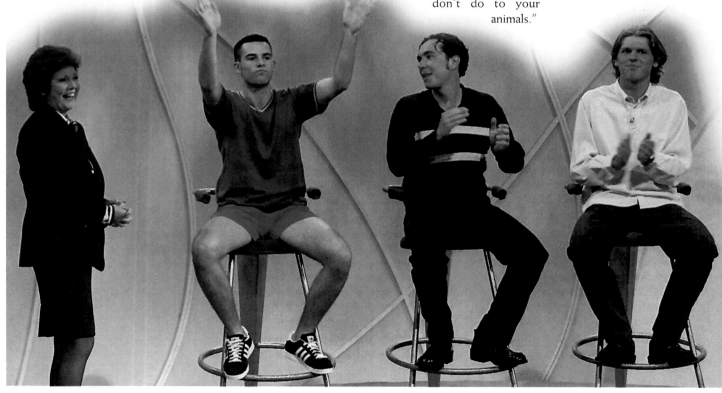

Lynda Bellingham

Lynda Bellingham is undoubtedly one of the best-known faces on television, the long running OXO advertisements have ensured that. But in her real home Lynda has much younger children and pets. Lynda told me how they came to own their dog Star. "At the time, I was playing James Herriot's wife in 'All Creatures Great and Small', where the storyline in one episode included a lovely Collie dog and its litter of five puppies. My son Michael, who was just four at the time, fell in love with one of the pups and we called him Star, because he was on the TV and had a white mark on his head. Our other family pet is a hamster we call Fudge, it's that sort of colour!

Lynda's career has had very few of the breaks that actresses suffer from. It's been hard work all the way. Pets have always played a strong part in her life. And her own son has been brought up with pets because of it.

"I think owning pets teaches children to be caring and responsible. Sometimes Michael may not want to take Star out on a wet windy morning, but pet ownership brings responsibility and the care is returned with unquestioning love."

Looking back, 'All Creatures Great and Small' has been one of the happiest episodes of her career to date. And the role of vet's wife came quite naturally to Lynda who is a farmer's daughter, she remembered those happy days for me, "It was a wonderful childhood, surrounded by all sorts of creatures. Father always had working dogs, such as Jack Russells, Terriers or Collies for the sheep.

"One funny thing happened during the lambing season, any little lambs that were too weak to stay with their mother we used to nurse in the house. In the kitchen we had a big Aga range with an open fire. We used to heat the oven up to round body temperature of 98 degrees

and place the baby lambs inside to keep warm. One afternoon our local vicar came round for a cup of tea, he was sitting next to the Aga passing the time of day

with my dad when out from the over came this whimpering bleat. His face was a picture when we opened the door and a live lamb peeked out, goodness

knows what thoughts were racing through his mind."

Lynda's childhood pets included a pony called Tiddlywinks, on which she won prizes at local Gymkhanas. But her love of riding ended with the onset of asthma. "I really loved my pony and was becoming quite a good rider, then at about 15 years of age I started sneezing every time I went near Tiddlywinks, the doctor said I had developed asthma and was allergic to the pony, so I stopped riding and never have since."

From OXO ads to the classics, Lynda Bellingham has played them all, and her most recent TV appearances have been with Amanda Redman and Sylvia Syms on the series 'At Home with the Braithwaites' and, with Jonathan Kerrigan, the romantic drama 'Reach for the Moon' as well as with James Bolam in the hit situation comedy 'Second Thoughts' which ran for five series. Her more serious roles, which she also relishes, have recently included Mrs Lupin in Charles Dickens' 'Martin Chuzzlewit'.

Johnny Briggs

It's a long way from smoky Battersea to the fields and farms of wealthy but windswept Windsford, Cheshire, but the generation that explored the countryside in their enforced isolation during the war years learnt a lot about how the other half lived. Johnny Briggs, born under the looming shadow of the power station in Battersea, learnt to love animals. "If you saw a cat with four legs in Battersea it was visiting!"

The war years were an animal-free zone in London but sunny Cheshire was a different matter. "Fluffy was my pet cat and the day he went missing was one of the worst of my life. But we found him the next day curled up in the linen cupboard with my socks! I used to go fishing as well, the only fish in London were at Billingsgate"!

We know Johnny best as the roguish Mike Baldwin from Coronation Street. "He's not like me at all," he says "For a start he has no pets. I've a dog called Daisy who looks like my childhood hero Lassie, plus a goldfish, a hamster and two cats. We are one big happy family and the Collie gets on wonderfully well with the children. I do think that some people get completely the wrong pet for their home. It worries me to see small children walking huge, great dogs, one good tug on the lead and they'd be over. I talk to my pets but the hamster is sulking because I forgot her birthday! I hope she forgives me soon."

At 12 the young Johnny Briggs was a talented young actor who won a scholarship to the Italia Conti Stage School where his music tutor discovered that Johnny could sing. He was on stage with 'La Boheme' at the Cambridge Theatre when Johnny was noticed by a stage producer. His first feature film was alongside Joan Collins in a gripping melodrama called 'Cosh Boy'. His National Service stint interrupted that career on the stage but not for long. Square bashing at Catterick Camp Johnny was tickled to discover that the first film showing in the unit's cinema was 'Cosh Boy'! "My Sergeant Major was not at all impressed."

After National Service Johnny resumed his acting career and

acquired his first dog – Whisky. "I loved that old dog. He turned circles of delight whenever he saw me. Then I won £25 on the premium bonds and decided to buy my mum a poodle. It was white, sweet and called Snowball. It was a lucky present. The next week I won another £25!

"Acting with animals has been a nightmare. I had to be persuaded on to a horse. I had a part as a Tax Collector and needed to ride a horse as part of the film. I was scared stiff of it. It was easily a foot taller than me and when the time came to try to mount I couldn't move for fear. Eventually they lifted me on and I was OK, but it took some doing!" After that first ride he took to it like a duck to water and now rides for relaxation.

He believes that the Brits take the biscuit for pet loving. The Americans tend to buy a dog for a purpose either to guard the house or for showing, or a Collie for farm work. But just having a dog for the sake of having a dog is not all that common. While filming in Alaska Johnny was concerned that a Husky dog would be cold living in the open and insisted that he share the crews living quarters. "The locals thought I was nuts!"

Frank Bruno

As former heavyweight boxing champion of the world, Frank Bruno is well used to delivering the knockout punch, and you wouldn't think to look at him that anything would give him a turn. As he claimed the title in 1995 from Oliver McCall, and faced Mike Tyson in the 1996 defence, he seemed all but invincible. But big Frank is the first to admit that a tiny Chihuahua can send him weak at the knees.

What scared of dogs – even one so small? Not all dogs, he has four fine specimens of his own. So does he have Boxers? He ought! Loveable Frank would rather get in the ring with his four pet Rottweilers than risk an attack from a little Mexican with attitude. You begin to get the feeling that he'd rather face another bout with Mike Tyson than go a round with a Yorkshire Terrier.

"I'm scared of small dogs because of an encounter when I was a kid", says Frank who doesn't scare easily.

"You have got to have respect for them, large or small – know what I mean! Even a little Chihuahua can bite, any dog can turn."

Frank certainly has respect for his four Rottweilers – 'Arry, Georgey, Bomber and Bruno. But in spite of their fierce reputation Frank doesn't think there is anything wrong with the breed.

"In fact I love them", he says. "They are really good friendly dogs. If you get them while they are young they are easy to deal with. I've had no trouble with them".

Frank has been an animal lover from the time he was a small boy.

"My first pet was Toby, a black and white cat. I liked him but all he wanted from me was feeding then he'd be off doing his own thing," remembers Britain's best-loved heavyweight.

As a result Toby was the only cat Frank has owned — he has stuck to his dogs ever since. He prefers their companionship. Cats are a bit too independent for him.

"I had this big Doberman called Bomber — he was my first dog. He was my friend and it broke my heart when he died at just eight years old."

Frank still remembers his canine companion having named one of his Rottweilers after him. As for 'Arry, any similarity with the boxing commentator Harry Carpenter is purely coincidental!

Frank, who started his boxing career when he got his first pair of gloves at the age of eight, knows all about the importance of training. He started serious sparring when he was 16 and the rest, as they say, is history.

And he agrees that training is just as important for animals as it is for humans. "My wife Laura took all four Rottweilers to obedience classes from an early age and now they respond to all the basic commands.

"Bomber tries to talk to me. When I say sit, he sits but then he starts barking as though to say 'If you say so Frank'…

As well as his four dogs, Frank has two horses, Diamond and Misty for his daughters Rachel and Nicola. "I like to go for long rides myself, especially when I go to Jamaica, Antigua or St Lucia," he says. "I like to ride up in the mountains and get away from it all."

So how is Frank wowing the crowds now? These days you are more likely to see Frank on the stage than in the ring. When he is back in Britain, Frank is well known now on the Panto trail – his Genie of the Lamp is legendary, a real scene-stealer. Not to mention trying to take on Harry Carpenter at his own game …

Malandra Burrows

As Cathy Glover in Emmerdale Malandra Burrows is always surrounded by all sorts of animals, as well as the wild foxes, squirrels, birds and hedgehogs that flock to her garden. She describes herself as an "avid animal lover". And at home, there's Roxy, the English Bull Terrier.

"She is the ideal family pet. I fell in love with English Bull Terriers because of Oliver Twist, Bill Sykes' dog is such a character. Roxy is so funny. They say that dogs take after their owners, well, I hope not! But I think she's beautiful. Though a lot of people say to me 'What have you got such an ugly dog for?'"

Malandra has always loved animals. "I had the usual pets as a child", she says. "There were a couple of goldfish that I fed on special flakes from the pet shop, a cat that was my constant companion and a little Yorkshire Terrier dog. I also set up a sort of insect hospital. I have never been scared of spiders or anything like that – in fact, I had a pet one. Once I found this ladybird that looked lost and took it home with me. Quite what the spider thought of it I don't know".

Malandra talks about the responsibility of having a family pet, "It's how they're brought up. They need responsible ownership and commitment. I wanted a dog that could come running with me", says Malandra. "I like nothing better

listens, obviously happy whenever I play the radio. I know it might sound daft but I do talk to her. She's full of fun and exactly the right kind of pet for me. I couldn't cope with a huge powerful breed and a little dog wouldn't be right either because they wouldn't be able to run with me. I think if people took more care of selecting a pet then there would be far fewer problems with unwanted strays."

Malandra has had some scary moments with the animals on the set of Emmerdale. "Cows frighten me," admits Malandra. "I think it goes back to when I was a child and I was scared of being kicked by them.

Anyway Cathy has to milk these cows on the farm and I just couldn't do it. Their tails swishing near me and the deep mooing was too much. I'd never make a milkmaid in a thousand years!"

But the thing that Malandra really can't stand is cruelty to animals. "They are such trusting innocent creatures that deserve our care not our abuse."

than being out in the field running with Roxy by my side."

English Bull Terriers have had a bad press recently and Malandra's love of Roxy is a testament to Roxy's sweet temperament. "She's a sweetie. My Roxy is like a child. I often

sing to her. Animals love music, especially Roxy. She sits and

Malandra returns to a theme that has cropped up again and again, that of responsibility. She concludes by saying that dogs should never be given as a surprise present, "Not for birthdays or for Christmas. It's just not fair to the dog or the person".

Beverley Callard

As Coronation Street's Liz McDonald Beverley Callard led the life from hell. First attacked by her husband, leaving her marriage in tatters, she then saw her son sent to prison and most recently falling for her husband Jim's physio, and leaving the street to set up a love nest at the other end of the country.

But now she plays a much more sober suited character as a bank clerk in BBC1's 'The Peter Principle' with Jim Broadbent. Life at home is completely different from both of these roles. Bev Callard, mum of two, has as her companions in the Bolton house, two gorgeous white Samoyeds.

Simba, who is a Leo, is the eldest – he's two years old and Keena, the younger of the two, he's only five months old and he's an Aries. The two Samoyeds are to replace a void in her life which was left by Sooty, her black poodle, who recently passed away.

A dog lover all her life, Beverley originally bought Sooty as a pet for her daughter Rebecca, but had found a devoted canine pal of her own.

"I'll never forget going to buy the puppy for Rebecca", says Beverley. Sooty was a treat for working hard at school. I said I was going to look at some antique furniture and came out with a little furry bundle of velvety black dog.

"Rebecca was so thrilled, she took one look at her and burst into tears. We really couldn't call her anything other than Sooty — it was the perfect name for her.

"The funny thing is we bought her for Rebecca but she followed me everywhere." Beverley obviously still misses Sooty."

But Sooty wasn't the first poodle that had found a place in Beverley's heart. She fondly remembers Pep, her first poodle with star quality.

Beverley says, "My little Pep was pure showbiz. If it ever rained — and let's face it, as you know in Manchester it rains a lot — she would not put a single paw outside. What a poseur she was! At night she'd sit right next to the television with an aloof look on her little face. I'm sure she believed we spent half the night watching her."

But the two Samoyeds are the current heart-throbs. Josh, Bev's 10 year old son, chose their names after seeing the Lion King. Josh wants to follow in the footsteps of his mum and his sister and become and actor. But Bev says, "He's only 10, so we'll have to see!

"Simba's very clever — he speaks on command and he'll sit and stay, I guess he wants to act too, but really they're a pair of laughing dogs. We thought they'd bring fun and laughter into our home and they wake me up in the mornings too."

Beverley has owned a number of breeds — not just the Poodles

and Samoyeds, both large and small. She believes that a dog's breeding and also its environment can be major factors in determining a dog's character.

She still remembers one particular pet she once owned

as a struggling actress living in Leeds. "I once bought a dog from a local pet shop. I'd been looking at its sad little face for days and in the end just had to buy it. I got it a lead, a nice red collar with a proper name tag and walked it home," she says. "We became friends on the way and she

seemed happy to be out of the window and into almost fresh air."

Sadly Bev's joy in Jingo (as she called the crossbreed Ridgeback) was to be short-lived. In spite of caring for her, taking her for long walks and doing everything that a pet lover could Jingo proved impossible to train.

"The vet said that Jingo had been abused as a puppy and it would take a long time to help her back from that trauma, remembers Beverley. "I was a young actress then and just didn't have the time needed for Jingo. It broke my hear to let her go, even though I found a good home with a nice family."

In spite of all her commitments – the hectic filming schedules, the three fitness videos and personal appearances – Beverley tries to spend as much time she can with her family and, of course, Simba and Keena.

Her other big love is her fitness. "I've done exercise for the past

20 years, it's a passion I have I can't let go. Coronation Street tended to take over your whole life but I've kept it quite separate and always will do. Along with my dogs, it helps to keep me sane."

"I've always been an actress and I've always been in fitness and I've always run the two side by side."

Through Coronation Street, her other recent successes and her various fitness projects Beverly has a very glamorous image, and she would never use cosmetics tested on animals. "Animals especially domestic breeds, place a great deal of trust in mankind," she says.

Beverley sounds the perfect dog owner, with a near perfect life that allows her to be with her dogs and children as much as she needs. What more could anyone want?

If you are lucky enough to have satellite or cable television, you already know Julia Carling's face very well. Currently on Granada Breeze successful co-hosting a spectacular show with George Hamilton. But everyone else will know her face a lot better as the year 2000 progresses. There are things in the pipeline for Julia that mean she will be a much more frequent visitor to our living rooms.

"Biff turned from a scatty little puppy into a wonderful friend and companion over that time of my divorce from Will about eight years ago. He was always there for me." Biff is a lively black Labrador, now eight years old.

"I've always been mad about dogs. The first dog I remember was rather strange in that it was a straight-haired poodle called Timmy. He was a real old stager. I remember him as a very old, deaf and blind dog when I was about three. He had been my father's dog before my parents married.

"Growing up in a family with dogs is good for teaching about responsibility. It also teaches you about communication in another language, whether it is cat, dog rabbit or horse. I learnt from my dog not to be selfish, that it's good to share. I have to admit that there was a time when I was completely mad about ponies. I had one until I was 17 and my ambition was to win the Burleigh Horse trials. I had mountains of rosettes. But when I left school I realised that it was my parents who would have to carry on with the hard work of looking after the horse and I decided that it was better if I didn't insist on having one again".

If it weren't Labradors for Julia, what would she choose? "One of the loveliest dogs I ever knew was a Labrador German Shepherd cross, which came from the German Shepherd Rescue. I love Scottie dogs for their character and Spaniels to. Irish Setters are there on the list but they do tend to be a bit loopy. I am very drawn to Boxers and Boxer crosses because they are so pretty, and Border crosses are beautifully lively. I'm not really fussy."

It must have been quite a surprise to find herself with Biff? "Biff is actually the only dog I have ever bought. Usually they came from rescue centers and that's what I would have preferred. But living in London I wanted to be sure that I had a dog I could rely on. I didn't want one whose history I didn't know, who might have run into traffic or caused an accident.

"Biff is a real Mummy's boy. He wakes me up in the morning by sitting on my pillow. Biff was a present from Will. We went to the Kennel Club for advice and they told us where to find the

best breeder and who had puppies that were registered with them. They were really helpful." She knew she wanted either a chocolate or black Labrador. And he has proved himself a friend indeed.

"He's in tune with all my moods. He just puts a protective paw on my shoulder as if to say 'Don't worry, I'm here'. He was the only thing that I insisted stayed with me after my divorce from Will. I couldn't see how I was going to survive without him and nothing else really mattered.

Julia is looking forward to her trip to Cruft's this year. Last year was her first ever visit, and as she puts it "My goodness, it is the place to find dog lovers. It was great to go. I had no idea that it would be so big or so organised." Julia was so impressed by the goods and services available to people with pets that she has decided to give quite a lot of thought to a special range of dog clothes and accessories, possible more, that she plans to launch fairly soon.

Her own "pet" charity is Breakthrough, which is a charity that's heavily involved in raising awareness about breast cancer. It is also committed to helping people who need counseling and support through illness. "It's a charity that I know does a lot of good in the community and I am very pleased to be able to do what I can."

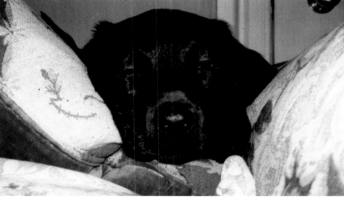

Does she think there have been changes for the better in our attitude to pets over the past few years? "That's a hard one! I remember the old dog licence, they rationalised its abolition by saying that it cost more to collect that the licence cost in the first place! I think it shouldn't have been abolished but raised to a sensible amount. Australia has just introduced

a dog licence of £50 with an extra £25 if the pet is unneutered. That could be the only way forward to make sure that pets are well cared for, but it will exclude many people from enjoying the company of a pet, that will always be a problem. For myself, I just can't imagine life without Biff.

If you were an avid collector of everything Dame Barbara had ever written you would need a shelf at least 12 feet long. If you wanted to collect every book ever translated into a foreign language, your shelf would stretch from here to Germany – her books are sold in every country in the world. If you wanted to amass every book ever sold your collection would number 700 million! No other writer has either written so many books or sold so many copies. So far, she has written 688 books, both fiction and non-fiction and its not over yet.

Her 98 years – she will be 99 this year - have seen more than their fair share of drama, but Dame Barbara Cartland and has never sat on the sidelines waiting for the world to come to her, she is there in the midst of life, always working hard, not only at her writing but also her social causes, her National Association for Health and her friends and family.

The best selling, most prolific author in the world also finds the time to be mad about dogs. And as she puts it, "Dogs have always been part of my life. My mother used to put the dogs in the pram with us when we were babies". Her own life is not that far away from romantic fiction except that it's true! Who was it said that fact could often be stranger than fiction?

Barbara Cartland

"I've done so many things in my life", she says with an obvious twinkle! Dame Barbara has always been besotted with dogs, as well as romance. Her own dog is treated to a diet of chicken, meringues and cups of tea.

"I've had hundreds of dogs throughout my life, and most are buried here. And I would like to be buried beside them in the garden."

Wogs was Dame Barbara's favourite dog, he travelled everywhere with her before she married and while her children were small. She says that she usually has both a small and a large dog together. But recently, their lovely black Labrador, Dickie, friend to their newest white Pekingese went missing while swimming in the Lake. "We kept hoping he would return, but that was months ago now. I'm beginning to think that someone may have stolen him. And I'd really much rather he were dead than kept by someone who would be cruel to him."

She says she tried cats as pets during her forties, but went back to dogs as soon as they moved to the country. "I do like dogs around me particularly the Pekingese because they are such charming companions and so full of character and life."

Her current companion is a white male, very unusual, called Tai Tai because royalty always called their dogs Tai Tai. "I sleep with him and he never wakes me up."

It's not been a cushioned or easy life. Her father died when she was 17 in 1917 in the final push for supremacy during the First World War and the family was left with no house, no money and no particular place to go. So her mother said to her "Where shall we go?" Her answer was simple - "London!"So that's where they went.

But they had already tasted poverty when her grandfather, who should have left the family a tidy fortune lost all his money in a railway scandal and took his own life.

Dame Barbara was a very pretty girl, a debutante presented at court at least twice, and was courted by, in her term "my men". She ran a hat shop near the Ritz in London but was so often invited to tea there that she spent most her time wearing the stock rather than selling it! "It was not a success." Then after 49 proposal of marriage from one particularly good-looking admirer she reluctantly accepted, at 25, wearing a creation from Norman Hartnell, "I was too young", she says now. And even the honeymoon in Paris and marriage to one of the richest men, Mr Alexander - Sachie - McCorquodale, couldn't make a success of it. But, Raine, her only daughter was later to be special confidante and step-mother to Diana Princess of Wales in her own fraught years.

Dame Barbara had to support both herself and her small daughter, during an age when it was definitely unusual, and writing kept her going throughout the years when Raine was small – 10,000 words a day. Her second marriage to Sachie's cousin, Hugh, was a much happier one, and led to romance and fidelity which would weave throughout her books.

Hugh McCorquodale was wounded at Passchendaele in 1917 when he was only 18 and not expected to survive, they thought that five years of marriage was as much as they could expect, but two sons, Glen and Ian and 28 years of happiness was the total. "My recipe for success was to have a second honeymoon every year". Each year, they returned to the Paris Ritz – "the most romantic hotel in the most romantic city" for their anniversary.

"My husband, Hugh, was always saying that the after-life was 'poppycock' but when he died in 1963 I had many strange experiences, that I am sure were him trying to contact me. It was the dead of winter and yet the house was filled with the scent of carnations, my favourite flowers, (pink ones filled our bedroom in the Ritz in Paris where we honeymooned in 1936). I am sure he was trying to tell me that he had been wrong."

She is justly proud of her good health. But all the women in her family, and it is definitely a matriarchal family, are long-lived. Her own mother was well over 98 when she died. And the glamorous trio of generations her mother Polly, Dame Barbara and Raine would enjoy making appearances together, usually connected with health issues.

Dame Barbara has written several health books which have been highly influential, particularly one about the healing power of honey, and has been well ahead of her time in promoting alternative therapies. Indeed her National Association of Health founded in 1964 was the first organisation to promote the use of vitamins.

Her life is testament to the idea that the writer must have a well-stocked mind and a well-stocked life in order to write. Her books always finish with the same words "They found love, real love which comes from God, is part of God and is theirs for eternity."

Wong was her favourite white Pekingese and her loyal companion for over 16 years. For him she wrote a poem.

For years you walked
beside me every day
For years you slept upon my bed
You showed your love in every way
I can't believe that you are dead.

If there's an after-life for me
Then I'd be lonely without you
I must be sure that you will be
With me, Whatever I may do.

So I pray to God who made you and me
Who in death swept us apart
To book a place in the Great to be
For a dog with a loving heart

Dame Barbara believes wholeheartedly in an after-life even for dogs. "Heaven wouldn't be heaven for me without dogs in it".

Pink is the colour that is always associated with Dame Barbara, for a different reason than everyone assumes. Pink is the most feminine colour, and Dame Barbara epitomizes femininity, but she acquired the colour plus a clear turquoise as "her" colours in 1922 while sitting on the bonnet of Howard Carter's car outside the newly discovered Tomb of Tutankhamen.

Suzanne Dando

There's a peach of a lady living in Peartree Cottage in a delightfully doggy village in the heart of the Cotswolds. It's Suzanne Dando, now well known as a sports present for Sky Television to top up her fame as a sports personality. She regards her finest hour as the time she represented Great Britain as captain of the gymnastics team at the 1980 Moscow Olympics.

There are two dogs, both Border Collies of good working stock, Moody and Blu, who has one startling blue eye. "Blu is a dream of a dog, easy to train and very responsive. That's what I like about Border Collies, you just have to say, 'Be Clean' and off he trots to the gutter to do his stuff." He is showing little sign of feeling his 12 years.

Blu was two when she acquired Moody, a bit more of a scatterbrain. And there's Ozzie and Pom, a pair of rescue cats with very unusual names, but not when you know that they belong to the one and only Bruce Roberts, who played Nick Parrish, the incredibly tall, dark and handsome policeman in the Australian soap "Home and Away".

They met when they were both starring in pantomime in Swansea. It was Sleeping Beauty and obviously Suzanne was playing Princess Aurora - the one who was a bit clumsy with the needle - to Bruce's Prince Charming. As she puts it,

"They kept saying to us, would we mind cutting that kiss down a bit at the beginning of the second act, we're running about ten minutes over!"

All that was at Christmas 1993 and they married for real in '94. "The dogs had been with me for all that time before we met, " she says, "yet they seemed to have met Bruce before somewhere. They just knew."

Sad to say, Bruce, Bru to his friends, was feeling desperately homesick for the wide open spaces of Australia and returned home last year. Suzanne is going too, as soon as she works out the best way forward for her beloved dogs. Blu is 12 and Moody 10 and Australia has quarantine laws like ours, not quite so draconian but daunting nonetheless. There is also a fairly hefty licence for each dog, but it's quarantine that is the problem.

"It's 60 days and for the first week you are not allowed to visit at all. Then you can only visit once a week. And they have all sorts of powers, even of destruction during that time. I don't think Blu could stand it. And I'm pretty sure I couldn't!" So they dawdle over to Oz in stages.

But if the Australia idea comes off, then Suzanne plans to fulfill her dream of a rare menagerie of dogs, cats horses, chickens and sheep, the lot.

"I'd indulge my passion for show jumping that I daren't when I was younger for fear of injury. Now I love to ride and am learning to instruct, purely so that I can improve. I'll never be top, but I want to be as good as I can be.

"I was born in Tooting, but moved to the Surrey countryside when I was about six months old. And almost the first thing that my mother did was to rescue this ball of fluff, a little ginger kitten who lived to be about 15. He was an incredible cat.

"Then we moved again to Sussex when I was about six. It was a huge new estate with lots of green fields around us. And one day my father said to my sister and me, 'Go and look in the kitchen'. We did and there was this tiny Beagle puppy. We called him Gus and he was a real Houdini, always escaping particularly when the local 'girls' were on heat."

From humble beginnings as the protégé of Ann Billingham, she went to gymnastic club in Brighton. But she really missed Gus when, at 14, her career as a gymnast started to take off and she was advised to go and live with an uncle and aunt near the gym in Lewisham, South London. She stayed there until she was 19.

"But on a Friday I would go home and Gus would always have rolled in something awful by way of welcome. And for when I got there, mum would keep Gus in the kitchen and tell me to hide so that Gus would find me! He never took long.

Ken Dodd

Happiness, Happiness, the greatest gift that I possess I thank the Lord that I've been blessed with more than my share of happiness.

Not for nothing has Ken Dodd chosen "Happiness" as his theme tune. It seems to sum up totally his attitude to life, a belief in jollity and God. His act is justly famous, the last of the variety men gives incredible value-for-money. Patiently waiting in the dressing room is his beloved Doodle the Poodle.

You hear the band strike up with a breakneck speed version of "Love is like a violin" and on to the stage, brandishing his ticklestick – scruffy of hair and merry of laugh – leaps the Professor of Ticklology, Ken Dodd OBE for another marathon of merriment and mayhem. He is one of the old school comedians and the better for it, who never pokes fun, hardly ever gets political, and is as happy as he seems. When so many of our comic heroes turn out to have a dark side to their characters, Ken practically stands alone. He is a "What-you-see-is what-you-get" comic, without any bitterness, moodiness and never any badmouthing. You can safely take your granny or maiden aunts. Not for him the droll sad-faced clown, it's a laugh a minute, and even the "unfortunate" episode with the tax office is treated with mischief rather than malice.

Despite his nice baritone voice, his semi-serious renditions of the old Music Hall and parlour songs, such as "Tears for Souvenirs" that always finish off his shows serve to emphasise the silliness of the rest of the act. For the songs, he would smooth is wild hair, but ruffle it back up into its normal mop as soon as the mood passed, never long. His shows are pure rib tickling mirth.

Ken has clocked up more than 50 years of mirth-making. Armed only with wit, a multitude of jokes and tickling stick he goes out to face his audience. His trademarks are tickling stick, diddymen, sentimental talk of hometown Knotty Ash, and those teeth and that hair. The teeth are insured for over a million pounds, the hair is definitely stranger to the brush!

He has a special place in my memories, I remember going to see him with my gran at the Manchester Palace Theatre when I was a little nipper in short trousers for my fourth birthday, and 30 years on I took my gran (long trousers this time!) to see him again. "You always get your money's worth!" you hear the audience muttering as they leave, still laughing. Once he gets on stage, the problem is getting him back off! His shows are famous for being marathons, an epic of five hours of rib ache is not unusual.

The biggest laugh is always at the expense of the tax people, "Fight organised crime — abolish the Inland Revenue" is one that has all the self-employed businessmen in the audience rolling in the aisles.

Fresh from his nationwide tour, Ken Dodd is still top of the laughter-maker's pops. He is reputed to be the last of the true variety men, the old Music Hall acts that toured Britain up until the 1950s. It's non-stop laughter that fuels him and his love of dogs, particularly his own Doodle, his black Poodle.

Has he always been involved with animals? "Animals are in my blood. There were three children, an older brother Bill and a younger sister June. It was a very happy childhood,

we had the best parents anyone could wish for. I remember wanting for nothing. My dad was a coalman, so there were the horses to look after, and we always had a tortoise — it always 'taught us' a lot!" Pause for laughter. "And dogs too. We had an assortment of dogs over the time we were growing up. We always had Fox Terriers, one I remember particularly was called Skippy. And then we had Boxers, very gentle dogs, that would eat anything and were particularly fond of us children." That was a bit

ambiguous and there's another uneasy pause for laughter! "Seriously though, he continues, "Boxers have always been a favourite and I wish the breeders could do something about their hearts, because they seem to be too heavy for them.

"Since 1960 I have been mad about Poodles. I was on tour in Torquay and "Love is like a violin" was at number one. I was passing a pet shop where the window was full of little poodle pups. I went in and bought one for my girlfriend.

he had a gift for names and he called him 'Touchet' in French to suit the dog, and I thought he was going to be a perfect little lapdog.

He was a terrible dog, always biting your ankles! I didn't know then that they were biters, and it has to be said that I was his Governor, no one else got a look in.

Doodle goes everywhere with me. He is always in the dressing room waiting for me to come off stage. Sometimes, he's on stage with me, making an unscheduled appearance. Well, people pop into the dressing room and leave the door open. He doesn't know he's not supposed to be there. He's usually on stage on the last night of the pantomime. He's a right poseur, loves to have his photo taken, and a real thespian, with brilliant timing for an entrance. He's a lovely and loving little dog who loves everyone.

Doodle is always welcome in the hotels we stay in, because poodles have wool instead of hair and virtually no one has an allergy problem with them."

Does cruelty upset him? There aren't so many strays in this country anymore but going abroad always reminds me what it used to be like. We were in Italy recently, and two puppies, hungry and cold, popped up through a drain in the middle of nowhere. We were about 20 miles between Sorrento and Positano and they weren't being looked after by anybody. We gave them all our sandwiches and

cakes, and then had to go. We went back a couple of days later, bashed a tin lid to find them and the poor little scrawny things came out to see us. The puppies were delighted to see us and the food and water."

What do his dogs mean to him? "I am quite happy to say that I love dogs. And I think that a subdivision of love should be "respect". I believe very strongly in God. God is the creator and I see God everywhere, God is in the grass growing, and God is in my little dog. Doodle is like my child. I don't have any children, but there's Doodle, and Herbert and Nellie my cats. I think that Doodle knows what is going on in my head, he licks the back of my ear to wake me up. When I am feeling not too 'robust' he just knows and comes to sit by me.

Ken Dodd has been rewarded with the OBE, for his charity work with

his favourites, the Water Rats, for whom he raises a vast amount of money. He is also reputed to be the favourite comedian of our much-loved "Queen-Mum".

What does he think about the hot topic of the moment, a dog register?

"We should never fear legislation, or interference. It seems to me to be better to have fewer animals and treat them better, and value them more."

Will he be going to Cruft's and what does he think about the dog showing world? Does he think it's cruel to have dogs in "beauty contests" such as Cruft's? Dogs, particularly show dogs are usually treated marvellously, I wouldn't mind swapping!" I don't really see the harm in even circuses. There are inspectors making sure that the animals are treated properly. I remember the old circus dogs. I don't think its degrading, or undignified for a dog to wear a hat and collar and make people laugh, I've done a lot of things far more degrading than that to earn a living!"

Everybody knows Noel
Edmonds – his is
such a well known face on
BBC1. But his love of his
family and his animals
including dog Tess is what
motivates him. And how
did it all happen?

The "baby boomer" generation
all remember huddling round the
radio to listen to "pop" on the
then brightest and best of radio
stations –Luxembourg. And it
was Noel Edmonds, a fresh
faced and chirpy 20 year old,
who kept us entertained with
what the BBC wouldn't play.
Now it is ironic that he is
regarded by the director of the
BBC Alan Yentob as the "most
important man in the BBC". He
took the riskier Luxembourg
career option despite an assured
place at University, but says now
with 20/20 hindsight "I'm far
better qualified for the life I've
led than university would have
made me".

He joined the BBC way back in
1969 and pretty soon was hosting
the Radio One flagship show
"Breakfast Time" for about 15
million listeners. But "Auntie Beeb"
finally realised that he was wasted
on the radio and he became a
regular sight on the little grey box
in the corner. The television
history that graces Telly Addicts is
rich as his own.

It could be said that he has single
handedly changed the social habits
of the nation. The death of the
national institution, "Saturday
Morning Pictures", coincided with
the first appearance of Noel's
innovative "Mulit-coloured Swap
Shop". It changed a nation's
viewing habits – and children all

Noel Edmonds

round the country refused to spend their Saturday mornings at ballet, gym, netball practice or swimming. At one time he was as ubiquitous as Carol Vorderman! He has been front man for most of the long-lived programmes such as Juke Box Jury, Top of the Pops, Top Gear, not to mention Telly Addicts and the House Party.

Despite this life in the limelight, Noel says that he is not as rich as reports suggest. "All I can say is that reports of my income are often vastly exaggerated – and that it's not as easy as it looks? Don't forget, Noel's House Party was live television. The amount of planning and professionalism that goes into it is immense. I'm certainly not the kind of guy who turns up, does the show and then spends the rest of the week on the golf course. I've never had time to learn golf!"

Unique Enterprises, which has given us institutions such as Mr Blobby and Crinkly Bottom, is Noel's company. Its interests are truly wide-ranging, and includes the Unique Broadcast Company which is the biggest of the radio programme producers, with about 12 programmes a week including the old favourites such as the Pepsi Chart show. So it's hard to see where he finds the time to see his family of three daughters and his animals.

The most important thing about pet ownership is that it teaches you responsibility," he says. "From the moment you have got something – a bird in a cage, a fish or a dog – it looks to you as a provider. I think it teaches children especially that we can all influence every living thing by caring a little bit more".

Noel lives in the heart of the country and admits to having built up quite a menagerie over the years. "We have three girls who are absolutely mad about animals", he says. "Living where we do is a pretty idyllic way to bring up children."

Idyllic or not Noel is very keen that their children grow up appreciating their pets. "There is more to it than just watching goldfish swimming around in a goldfish bowl. I want to educate my children to be responsible. They love ponies and they all work hard to ensure the ponies welfare."

Noel's love of animals developed early. As an only child in Ilford, Essex his best friend was called Sooty and was a black cat". It was a real family pet and I think it stayed longer with the family than I did. "If you are an only child I think that it matters immensely to have a pet. I think you learn responsibility and appreciate affection, both taking and giving it.

As well as the children, the ponies, the donkey, the dogs and the five cats, there's Noel's favourite, Tess the Border Collie.

"She runs our life," he jokes. "We do have some dogs on the estate who work the sheep but that seems to be beneath Tess. She's very much the executive model."

Noel used to own Great Danes and came to Border Collies rather late, but better late than never. And the thing that stands out about Borders is their quick thinking intelligence, "a bit of a contrast to the Great Danes!" I think he said something about their being "less intelligent than a building brick" or something like that!

Border Collies need lots of space to play and run and with Noel's family she has not only those things but also lots of other people to play with. "She really is part of the family. She organises the children and tries to herd them up at times."

Something that every Border Collie owner would instantly recognise is the need to have something in the mouth. "She never goes anywhere without something in her mouth."

At eight years old, a bit young really Tess is starting to suffer from arthritis, "but we have a good vet who is looking after her." And after a series of injections she is showing signs of improvement.

One area that Noel feels strongly about is pets and the law. "I am not a fan of too much legislation but I care about my family. Since I include the animals in my family, it is very natural for me to care about animals. I just believe that it all comes back to the word 'responsibility'. It all comes down to accepting the fact that here is a living creature and generally speaking you are responsible."

Everybody know
Russell Grant, he'
simply the most famou
astrologer in the wester
world. He is an Aquariar
born in Middlesex, wh
moved into "media circles
and was invited to writ
his first magazine colum
for the monthly societ
magazine, Tatler. Then h
moved on to be residen
astrologer for the T
Times, the biggest sellin
magazine in the country
And many people give him
sole credit for th
popularity of astrology i
Britain today.

He is now hot on the trail of th
tempting holiday programme
that litter our screens at th
moment. His short and swee
"Postcards from…" for Channe
5 is based on his successful serie
of "real countries" books.

Russell's interest in dogs is no
so well know, he has two dogs
Owen a Labrador and Dolly,
mutley, who get on very wel
together. "Owen is still going
strong, he is 10 years old now
and still as Taurean as ever. The
there's Dolly who's our mongre
— we got her from the RSPC/
about two years ago and she'
vitality plus!"

But his interest in animals whe
he was a child started with cat
rather than dogs. "My first pe
was a black cat, which I bough
when I was on tour in Blackpoo
which would be 25 years ag
now. But my grandmother wh
died last Easter had lots and lot
of pets. She had budgies an

dogs — Cocker Spaniels especially and Gundogs. So that's where I got really involved with pets."

We all know that Labradors make lovely family pets, but is that why he chose Owen? "I love their friendly nature, they're warm and affectionate, more than anything though it's their soppiness! They flop around and like to be with you. I just love their faces, they're very handsome dogs. My love of Labradors was purely because of my grandmother, I was brought up with them, so they're familiar and therefore have a security attachment."

Yet Russell confided that Labradors don't really suit his personality. "My mongrel Dolly, who's a bit Whippet and a bit German Shepherd, is more like me. She's zippy and fast, whereas Owen is more relaxed and doesn't want to do anything at any pace whatsoever. Because he is so relaxed, he's just sort of there in the room when you are, giving you that feeling of relaxation and calm.

"But Owen has his own unique appeal. He's not like other Labradors I've known in

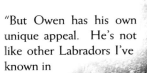

the past. And Dolly is totally unique — if she comes into the bed she likes to go straight under the bedclothes and not be seen, she likes to hide underneath them. If you uncover even her tail she wants the duvet to cover her completely."

Recently it has seemed that there are more cats in British households. There are about eight million cats and only about seven million dogs, and the decline in dog ownership seems to be continuing. Had he seen this coming and how does he account for it?

"Cats are less responsibility. Basically you can go away and leave a cat for a couple of days. I think that a cat's more independent, so therefore less of a responsibility than a dog would be, unless you're the sort that wants to go away and take your dog with you. I would say that that's possible the reason.

"Certainly I wouldn't have an animal at all if I thought I couldn't take care of it. I would look around and see if there were any children in the home — because dogs can be very upset.

If people are looking for animals, don't go for pedigrees necessarily — but go to the RSPCA or People's Dispensary for Sick Animals, there are lots of lovely animals.

"Dolly came from the RSPCA and she would have been without a home. She's the most wonderful animal and I miss her a great deal when I'm away. Also I've noticed that she doesn't suffer with all the ailments that my Labrador does."

Does he do horoscopes for dogs? "I wouldn't think it would be appropriate. Serious readings need a lot more information than you can usually supply for dogs, so I would give it a miss!"

Rolf Harris is a regular sight in our living rooms, and has been welcome there for over 25 years, since the early days of those glorious larger than life paintings, "do you know what it is yet?" I for one, couldn't work it out for ages, it was always back to front, or oddly angled but always HUGE! Rolf has boomeranged from art to photography, from number one records and on to our screens as presenter of BBC1s Animal Hospital.

Animal Hospital is now six years old and, even for the squeamish, is compulsive viewing. Rolf's presentation style is beautifully warm and witty, yet openly emotional, and it is now difficult to imagine how anyone else would tackle what must be an exacting role. He is often moved to tears at a sad story, but can be equally cheerful when things go right. But most particularly he is, in his words, "a mediator, a demystifier" and has proved a very valuable asset in the role.

What kind of pet would he choose in an ideal world? "I think a cat or a dog is best because they are closest to us in their affinity.

"I'm definitely not a horse person! I have bad memories of the farm back in Australia, when I was about 11 years old a friend plonked me on a horse to toughen me up, and then, like kids do, slapped it on the

Rolf Harris

bottom. We got off to a racing start but then something spooked it and it stopped dead on a sixpence, and I went over the top.

"That was almost my last experience with a horse – then at about 40 I was doing a scene with a stage coach and a runaway horse fell and almost wrecked my leg. I'm a bit scared of horses. Always a bit tentative". His own pets number three. He has two Devon Rex cats, which are large, friendly and unusual. "They always want to be with you, and behave more like dogs. They follow you everywhere and want to stand on your shoulders. Sit down and they're on your lap, and they're also quite greedy. The mother is called Beatle and the son, a big ginger one, is Toffee."

He also has a black Standard poodle called Summer. "Why Summer?" Simply because we got her in the summer! And although there isn't a lot of time my main thrill is to walk her on the downs at home."

Rolf's career has been a rare mixture. And Animal Hospital was a completely new departure for him, what does he think is the appeal? "I think it's that the programme uses real people, real vets, real pets and no actors. There are no scripts and no learnt lines. And the people involved have been able to ignore the cameras. If

people are doing a job they like, they are happy with the cameras and the paraphernalia.

"It's like a London taxi driver, quite happy to talk about everything and everyone, but put him in a studio with lights and glare and cameras, and I've watched people completely clam up."

And his own part he feels is important in putting people at their ease. "The people I meet at the hospital have seen me all their lives, I'm Rolf, I'm definitely not Mr Harris, just a friend. Sometimes I question the vet on

their behalf as a go-between, to take away the tension, panic and pressure. Some owners are scared stiff about what happens. We had a lady the other day, she was petrified, and wanted a nurse to hold her dog while he had his stitches removed. She

was absolutely terrified of the pain involved. I calmed her down and explained that there is no pain. I was there to hold her hand, as it were, and she coped amazingly. It always helps to have a friend with you.

"Also I love animals, and I think it is important to have someone there to demystify the whole thing. Animal Hospital is basically about animals, and you never know what's coming in. One day it's a cruelty

case. Animals come in which have been brutally treated and neglected. It's heartbreaking but it teaches people what to do, and also the penalties for not doing it right. It's really just about dispensing advice and information about keeping pets."

Rolf has obviously learnt a lot from Animal Hospital, and he says that it is chiefly a learning tool "Though I hope that, sometimes, people learn what NOT to do. Though the cruelty and neglect cases that we see are really grueling, it is important to show them. It's what the RSPCA is about."

And his advice to pet owners his think twice before getting any kind of pet. "There are always going to be costs involved, such as vets, injections and neutering – it's not just a once only deal, the ongoing costs can be huge." Rolf has heard more than his fair share of horror stories. And people do learn what not to do as well as the right way to treat animals.

"But it seems to me that, more often than not, it's carelessness and not a deliberate act that causes a lot of the problems for animals. For example, an unneutered bitch that is allowed to go out on its own and mates with a much bigger dog causes an immense amount of suffering for her and people leave it too late to sort out the problems and it can cause the death of the bitch if the puppies are too big to be born. I've seen it time and time again.

But my own pleas is that people stay with their dog at the end,

and not be frightened of it. I remember Barney, the vet's dog who was suffering so much and his quality of life was really bad. His eyesight had gone, he wasn't eating, couldn't walk and his bladder and kidneys weren't working properly. I went in with the vet to see what happened at the end, hoping to be able to ask the right questions and make it easier for people to understand what really goes on. I ended up in tears, but it certainly helped me and I think it helped the vet too.

"You see people in the waiting room, they come in with their dog, but the dog is walked or carried into the vet's back room and that is that. You ought to be with them at the end, for you as well as for them.

"I feel very strongly that people should no what happens when

the owner has to make that awful decision."

Which are the popular pets back home in Australia?

"The popular pets in Australia are the dogs. There is certain amount of anti-cat feeling among naturalists because the cat is such a brilliant killing machine. Cats tend to live outside and go feral, that's the macho thing among the Aussie population – there's no mollycoddling – and the cat has destroyed so many of the indigenous creatures. It has been introduced and grown up in an area with no predators except the Dingo. There was a popular bumper sticker among naturalists that says 'The only good cat's a flat cat'.

Rolf tells a story of a particular water hole near where he lived

in Australia which was full of the remains of local wild birds. The local cats had entirely destroyed all the wildlife and in among the bones of the birds, they found some cat bones. Having killed everything that came to drink the last cat had starved to death.

Rolf has been associated with so many different avenues, with rock albums, painting and photography, MBE and much, much more. So where next?

"I would love to do some real animation like Rolf's Cartoon Club, I would love to set aside a couple of years to do that, an animated film. But you have to be so dedicated and spend about 24 hours a day for two or three years at least. And at the moment, I'm very happy with my role of Animal Hospital."

Tim Healy

Tim Healey has spent his acting career as anything from builder to butler. He recently finished a stint of 'butling' on our screen as Jacob Collins, the maitre d'hotel of the Grand, the series on ITV of the life and times of a rather lively northern hotel.

You will probably remember Tim Healey from "Auf Wiedersehen Pet", "King Leek", "Common as Muck", and more recently from John O'Sullivan writer of "Only Fools and Horses", there is "Heartburn Hotel", a new series on BBC1. But as well as acting and singing he has a head full of memories of his motley assortment of childhood pets – mice and budgies, cats and dogs. He is now mad about Boxer Dog Sadie.

Your very first pet, no matter how big, always has a special place in your heart and when it dies there is an enormous sense of loss. Tim is definitely no exception to this rule. "My first pet was a budgie called Bobby when I was about six or seven years old – he was brilliant! He used to fly down and knock all my toy soldiers down. I used to line them all up and open the cage and Bobby used to come and knock them all down. Sadly I remember when it died – poor little thing – my mam jammed it in the door – it was following her into the kitchen and she shut the door. I remember it was the first big crisis of a pet dying in the house."

He knows how much that lesson taught him about the care that pets need and the things they teach us about responsibility, but it seems to have jogged his memory about the other tragic tales in his childhood.

"And I had mice I remember, that's another tragic story! I remember I was going to school one day and I'd had my wellies in the front of the fire and the mice had about 12 little babies running about the flat and I thought I had put them all back in the cage but one of them must have got in to my wellies. I had no idea and I walked back to school in my wellies and I felt something – and there was this dead mouse, I remember picking it up and bursting into tears and the whole class were jumping up onto the chairs.

"When I was 11 we got Smartie, a Corgi. He was a great big one, like an Alsatian with no legs. He was two years old when we bought him.

"My brother had a brilliant dog called Joey, a huge brown and black Border Collie, when he was in the Royal Marines – and it became the Royal Marines' mascot. It was incredibly well trained and lived on the army camp when he was on tour of duty in Britain. But when he went abroad, and spent a lot of time in Northern Ireland, I used to look after him."

But now the whole family, Denise Welch who plays Natalie Barnes behind the bar in the Rover's Return in "Coronation Street" and son Matthew are devoted to their Boxer dog Sadie.

As often happens, it was son Matthew who badgered his parents for a dog. They were very fussy about what sort they had and everyone had their own ideas. Someone in the family had to make a decision and find the perfect breeder, treading through the minefield of everyone's prejudices and predilections.

Finally though, it sounds as if the decision to get a Boxer was carefully reached one that was made in committee with the whole family. "Boxers have got a wonderful temperament, very placid and not aggressive and quite faithful – I now that some of them can be a bit goofy and daft but I was sort of limited as to what I could bring back, but I knew the family wouldn't let me in without something with four legs.

"She was the last one of the litter, that's why she's not so big, and I felt so sorry for her. There had been six or seven in the litter but she had been left all on her own. The funny thing was she sort of locked on to me. She watched me go all the way past, then I walked back again and she quietly watched me all the time. The look she gave me was as if she was saying to me, 'I'm the one for you, you know'.

"Sadie is two years old now and a marvellous dog. She was about four months old when we got her and really she was a bit on the small side. And she wasn't very confident when we first had her. Now she's turned into a great dog."

There have been some recent studies done in America that show that if children have access to a pet early on life, it teaches them the rules of maintaining good relationships. Is he glad to be starting his own youngster off in the way of life with pets?

"Matthew treats Sadie like his little sister, and she's still a little baby. He knows that animals aren't toys and he respects that."

His career has been an interesting mixture. "I've been very lucky – in that I started my career with a little theatre company – and we just did new plays by new writers and I did dozens of them."

Tim is always busy, yet we rarely see him on our screens since his big successes. He prefers theatre, "Because it's an instant reaction and it's immediate and it's new. TV is a completely different art form – if you're doing something in the theatre that's funny you get an instant reaction. If it's sad, people cry in the audience whereas if you're playing it to a camera you have to wait. So you question your performance the whole time – and wonder if it is funny or moving. You don't get that in theatre – the audience let you know honestly what they believe or what they think. And it's a buzz. But financially you're often better off in TV than theatre."

But Tim's favourite piece of work was for television way back in 1980. "It was called the World Cup' and its about the first ever Football World Cup, all based on a true story. Apparently it was won by a little team called West Auckland, all miners from County Durham. They beat Juventus! They basically came back from Italy with the World Cup and went back down the pit. They got time off work without pay". This piece combined most of his many passions – football, acting and the north.

The big break for Tim was "Auf Wiedersehen Pet" for ITV. "It probably launched me, giving me the chance to do all these other roles that I'm doing – so that was another very important job. Billy Ivory is a writer who I'm very keen on, he wrote 'Common as Muck' too – and then a film called 'King Leek' and I think that's the first time I've had something written for me. That is very special. There's another writer friend of mine, called Tom Halliway, who I've done a lot with, not so much on TV but as a playwright in the theatre. He's done a lot of fantastic stuff – probably about half a dozen of his plays that

Gloria Hunniford

Gloria Hunniford's life has been surrounded by pets, children and happiness. About 16 years on Radio 2 has kept her in the public eye, and a few more years behind her in radio generally, as well the years of presenting a variety of TV shows. She is a regular and welcome face on TV, instantly recognisable and seemingly quite happy to move over when her daughter Caron Keating – of Blue Peter fame - wanted to try the limelight. Mother and daughter make a winning combination, and it's a real wonder no one has thought of teaming them together!

Yet few people know that her warm Irish heart is full to the brim with the homely love of animals, mainly dogs. The unexpected death of her Retriever, Remy has been made easier by the presence of 10-year-old Honey the Poodle.

"Though my father would never allow us to have dogs at home when we were small. They would have disturbed the birds." Her father kept racing pigeons and her pet in childhood was a beautiful white dove called Sparky. "We would get on our bikes and go for miles. There was Dad with his pigeons and me with the picnic. He would let the birds fly off and it always amazed me how they could find their way home."

As soon as she had children of her own, Gloria kept dogs. One Labrador clearly has stayed in their minds for many, many years. Some dogs make such an impression. "Che the Labrador was a present for my son Michael when he was eight and was really the grandfather of the house. We brought Che over from Northern Ireland specially. And Michael grew up with him as a playmate. For 18 years we looked on him as part of the family, a proud old gentleman whom we all loved. Just before Christmas '94 he started getting weak and there was nothing more the vet could do. I cried for days out of love and compassion I had to take the advice of the vet, who painlessly put him to sleep. It's the saddest thing when a pet dies, but there is no merit in allowing them to suffer. You have to know when it is time to say goodbye and be strong enough to allow it. You have to think of the good of the dog."

"Remy we will miss for different reasons. It's so hard when a pet dies. You remember all the others you have loved and lost. But I'm pleased we still have Honey. And who knows, very soon we'll have to start thinking about topping up again with some more dogs! One just doesn't seem enough."

Gloria currently can be seen on weekdays on Channel 5 presenting her magazine programme called 'Open House'.

Michael Le Vell

There have been wedding bells in the life of Michael Le Vell recently. Not for him but for his Corrie character – Kevin Webster. Steamy scenes for the simple mechanic - the man at the centre of an increasingly bitter love triangle, you wonder how he has the stamina to continue!

As Coronation Street's possibly unlikeliest love rat, he had the whole country debating the rights and wrongs of his decision to leave wife Sally behind with two young children.

But away from the small screen, actor Michael Le Vell is only too happy to leave all the controversy behind and retire to the country whom he shares with his wife, fellow actress Jeanette Beverley, and the canine love of his life - German Shepherd Zak. Goddess was Zak's companion who very recently died at a ripe old age.

With action hotting up in his Street life, it's the ideal retreat for Michael. After all what could be a better way to relax than a walk in the country with your canine pal.

"When it's been hot on the set and the lines have been hard to learn I can get out into all that fresh air with my dogs," says Michael. "Goddess always seemed to know when I was coming home. My wife Jeanette says he recognised the sound of my car and sits behind the door waiting for me to come in.

"Half an hour in the fields with the pair of them used to blow all my cobwebs clean away."

Michael and Jeanette – you may know her from the drama series Children's Ward – are like many couples who care a great deal about their pets, they have developed an almost telepathic link with their dog.

This is particularly noticeable around holiday times.

"We start packing weeks in advance", says Michael, "or at

least Jeanette does. No sooner do the cases come off the top of the wardrobe than the dogs know we are going away. It can last for ages, Zak gives you this 'Please don't leave me' look and Goddess used to stand at his side, all soppy and sad.

"I often wonder how they knew, but they did."

The two German Shepherds had very distinct and different personalities.

"Goddess was just like me," laughs Michael. "She was hyperactive and into everything. If the paper pops through the door it's a race for who gets there first. If Goddess won, we could forget the front page!

"Zak on the other hand is so laid back and at ease with the world, like Jeanette. It's almost as if our dogs imitated us. Goddess was me and Zak is Jeanette.

"If we ever disagree about something, like watching football on the telly, then up walks Zak and sticks a great paw on my lap. It's as if he is keeping the peace, it really makes us laugh."

Indirectly animals and wildlife have played a major part in furthering Michael's professional career.

As a youngster he played a major role in his Manchester comprehensive school's production of Kes in which a young boy befriends a Kestrel. He so impressed his teachers that they steered him to a

professional career. Once again the play was Kes and this time the director sent Michael to falconry school to learn about kestrels for his role.

"It was great fun for me", he says, "though at first I was frightened. The birds have huge wing spans and when they come in to land on your arm it can be scary. One thing it did teach me was not to flap in such situations. I leave that to the birds."

One of Michael's first TV roles was in the zoo series One to One. He played a keeper and was sent to a real zoo to discover how the job is really done.

"I'd just fed the lions and tigers, scrubbed the crocodile's back with a soft brush and was cleaning out the brown bear's pit

when a mighty paw raised the iron gate leading out of the cage

"I still don't know how Bruno did it, the thing should have been locked. But this huge creature lurched out and rumbled forward it my direction. They are bigger than you think believe me, and fast too. I dumped the sack I was carrying, dropped the brush and was out of the pit double quick.

"When I told the director what had happened he seemed really pleased. He said something like 'what a super experience, now you know how it feels to be frightened for your life'."

Having been a Street regular for many years, Michael has managed to steer clear of much involvement with animals.

Madonna

❝ **Mirror, mirror on the wall, who is the best-selling female artist of them all?** ❝

The answer is obvious – Madonna Louise Veronica Ciccone, the biggest selling female artist of all time. With vital statistics, like 12 million sales of "Ray of Light", under her belt, and many more songs and films, and books in the pipeline she has proved her classic status.

Madonna, mother to little Lourdes, has three dogs in the family. Pepito is her longest standing pet, an American Pit Bull Terrier. She also has an apricot Shih Tzu and a new addition, her little Chihuahua bought specially for little Lourdes.

The self-styled "Material Girl" is a well-grounded business woman with a clear and honest grasp of what makes the world tick. Her company Boy Toy will ensure that she never starves, and Lourdes is being brought up to understand the value of the good things in life.

As the material girl became maternal girl, she shocked most of us. Madonna has come to the responsibilities of motherhood relatively late. As a multifaceted individual, she looks like making a complete success of her other concerns.

The announcement from the set of Evita that she was pregnant was to some people almost as surprising as when her namesake announced the very same thing! But as she points out, "I'm not the first person to attempt to bring up a child without being married. People are extremely judgmental of me and my choice to have a child and not be married as if I were the first person to do it. For some reason I'm being held up as an anti-family symbol. I know lots of married people who have terribly unhealthy relationships and marriage isn't a guarantee of anything". Although the relationship with her personal trainer, Lourdes father Carlos Leon has sadly disintegrated, she is still in touch with him on a daily basis.

Madonna admits quite candidly that she was late to motherhood because as a child and teenager

she was expected to look after her father's new family of babies in Michigan where she grew up. Madonna's mother died when she was only six, and her father remarried soon after. "I was very wounded by her death. But while I suffered a great deal, it also freed me in a lot of ways. Freed me perhaps, in the kind of parent I could be."

There were seven smaller brothers and sisters. Madonna was the obvious baby sitter. In fact she was given the responsibility for most of the family chores. "You name it, I did it," she says. "Defrosting the freezer, babysitting, vacuuming. I was not in a hurry to get tied down!"

Stability for Lourdes comes from Madonna's decision to put work on the "back burner" until the child is ready. Lourdes and Madonna are often seen out together. Lourdes, known as Lola, for one so young doesn't need any tips from her mum on how to stay in the limelight, she stole the show.

Shock tactics and pure unbridled talent have maintained Madonna at the top of the tree. Where other artists remove their older material from the record shop shelves in order to introduce new albums, Madonna's continue to sell. Madonna has the ability to re-invent herself as often as is necessary in order to become a lasting force.

Since 1984, from "Like a

Virgin" to "Ray of Light and beyond, through about 45 singles and 12 albums the progress is unmistakable and also shows a good grasp of her changing market. Where singles used to sell to her fans and devotees, "pop", we are all growing older together and it is now albums with classic tracks that tend to appeal.

Responsibilities now include the care of her new man, Guy Richie (Director of the acclaimed 'Lock, Stock and Two Smoking Barrels'), Lourdes and her family of dogs. "Sadly most American Pit Bulls are no strangers to publicity – most of it bad. Under the Dangerous Dogs Act 1981 in Britain it is illegal to breed them. Each one has to be registered and neutered." But Madonna isn't put off. She gives Pepito – lucky dog! – a kiss, and says " I believe that it's the owners who give the American Pit Bull a bad name. Macho men use innocent dogs as an extension of their manhood."

In fact she is convinced that it is Pepito who keeps her feet so firmly on the ground. "Fame is something that has happened to me. In fact, the Madonna you see on MTV or in the films is the 'other' me. The real me has good days just like everyone

else. There are days when the dog eats my best shoes …"

It's east to forget in the amazing success of her recording and song-writing career that Madonna is also a talented actress and film star. She showed her mettle in her professional attitude to her latest role in which she was cast – unfortunately now shelved – for "50 Violins". She has learnt how to play the violin – look out Vanessa Mae!

Success with the film version of Andrew Lloyd Webber's 'Evita' used her talents well and she says that it was the role she relished. "I had always admired Eva Peron – she was a woman who knew her own mind, knew how to get her own way, and was admired for her dignity." It is perhaps inevitable that Madonna and Eva Peron should be compared. The myth has grown up the both came from humble beginnings on the "wrong side of the tracks" yet the differences are obvious straightaway.

Madonna was brought up in the relative comfort of a middle-class Italian home, with a strict regime, warmly administered. Also Madonna, unlike Eva, didn't need a man to help in her search for status. Eva needed "The Colonel" but Madonna has, possibly helped by the "girl power" spirit of the age, gone it

Doing a George Michael is a well-known phrase in the music world meaning being someone who has been able to progress from "teeny bop" dance music idol into the adult world of the mature singer songwriter.

How much of the transition into a mature artist, and a mature person, does he owe to the love, loyalty and lifelong friendship of his dog Hippy.

George Michael was born on 25 June 1963, the son of north-west London Greek-Cypriot parents, and started life as Georgios Kyriacos Panayiotou, and, as he puts it, "Though George Michael takes over on stage, I spend most of my time as Georgios".

George Michael hates being interviewed and hates his photo taken. Yet he needs no introduction to most people. His elder sister Yiolda still calls him Yog, the name Wham-mate Andrew Ridgeley bestowed on him when they first met at the age of 12. He acquired the "George" from the rest of his class mates at his north London Comprehensive. It stuck.

"Andrew and I met at school. We had the same sense of humour. But really when I look back I think we were so cocky and childish."

They are reputed to have become firm friends after a playground fight was suddenly forgotten when they discovered that they were both huge Elton John fans. In his turn Elton John

George Michael

has called George Michael "The greatest songwriter of his generation".

Though Andrew and George went their separate ways in 1986 they are still friends. Andrew Ridgeley was very sporty, in constant confusion about whether to be a pop star or a professional footballer. George had no qualms – he had been a budding pop star since the age of seven when he was first introduced to the music industry by way of a tape recorder. It was hardly ever silent, and George's mind was made up.

The violin was his first instrument, and the piano, but a neighbour heard him singing one morning and remarked to George's mother, "Hasn't George got a lovely voice". The rest, as they say is history!

Though George would rather be remembered as a songwriter – "I want people to still be singing my songs in 30 years" - his voice is unmistakable.

The Panayiotou family was very close, and very

strict. George's mother Lesley helped his father in their restaurant, and sisters Melanie and Yiolda were also part of the kit. His father – always known as Jack - watched the only son's progress in the music industry with an open mind. Though a loyal supporter, in 1983 he was heard to remark, "It won't last six months".

George understood his father's misgivings. "Dad thought the pop world was really lax – full of layabouts. But when he saw how hard we worked, he got more reasonable."

Andrew and George's first attempt at a band – The Executive – ended in failure. George remembers that the band "had a problem with remembering to turn up!" They did cover versions of Andy Williams "Can't Get Used to Losing You". George was earning his keep as a DJ in a restaurant in north London – and hating to be in the limelight. "I used to break out in a cold sweat just talking to about 60 people. I sometimes wonder how I got to where I am."

Wham! was born one chilly night in 1982 and didn't have to wait long until they came of age. Like the name, their songs were crisp, bright, catchy and full of rhythm. It made a huge impact in its three short years, and the videos and the dance routines also had their impact. They were two good-looking hunks who had an appeal for both men and women, and the teenagers swooned and screamed. George was as fit as he's ever been. A tendency to put weight – since school day diet

of peanut butter and jam sandwiches were replaced by an on-stage workout every night. 'Fantastic' was the first album – through 'Make it Big' – to 'Music from the Edge' of heaven and 'Wham! The final' in 1986 and then it was all over the bar the shouting? But was it?

Even in the days of Wham! if George Michael fancied a slow number – such as Careless Whisper – the usual dance beat up-tempo rhythm of Wham! wasn't the right setting for it.

As time passed it became clear that George Michael was taking

on more and more of the musical responsibility of Wham! and Andrew's role within Wham! became more and more unclear. They decided that a split was inevitable, though no blood was spilt.

The two men behind Wham! went their separate ways in 1986 — Andrew Ridgeley to a small village in Cornwall and George to an international jet setting lifestyle that appears to suit him very nicely.

Now it seems that George Michael shares his time between court battles and walking his dog on Hampstead Heath. Certainly there have

been many litigious episodes — at the very start of it all they discovered the name Wham! already belonged to an American Punk duo who promptly sued.

George Michael's solo career started as it meant to go on with huge success. Faith, the first solo album, had sales of 16 million worldwide — multi-platinum in record terms. As an album it was long-awaited and welcome. Its dedication says a lot about George Michael's maturity. "These songs are the result of the last

two years of my life. They are dedicated to my family and friends, whose loyalty and time are more important to me than ever before. Love as always."

'Faith' stayed at number one in the British album charts for 72 weeks, and top spot in the US for four weeks. It was the album in 1990 'Listen without Prejudice Volume 1' that Sony "took against". It looked as though George Michael and Sony would have to part. Fortunately, after a six-year court battle that he lost, Virgin and Dreamworks took over his contract and released him from his self-imposed embargo on more songs.

Now he is flavour of the month again and Sony are happy to re-release his work. "Older" in 1996, wasn't well received in the States but was very much appreciated in Europe. It was Virgin record's fastest-selling album ever.

1998 was a bad one for George Michael. His mother died after a battle with cancer, and he was privately getting on with his life and his friendships when the storm broke over his arrest in Los Angeles. The court case doesn't seem to have affected his long-term affability. Short-term it may have harmed him. He told Michael Parkinson in a ground-breaking television interview that "It was my father and an old friend of my mother's who put it all in perspective for me. They just said ' You've just got to get on with it.' And so I did."

Yet it is quite difficult to get to know the man

behind the stardom. Not many people know that after his bad year it was his father and his dog Hippy, a yellow Labrador, that he relied on for support.

What does his dog mean to him? "Hippy is always happy to see me. I know that he sits by the door waiting for me to come home. When I am home we go for long walks together as often as I can."

Hippy the dog stays in London with his family when he has to visit the States — he seems to have a dog Stateside as well — and Hippy sits waiting for "His master's voice" to come on the radio or television and he reacts with a happy wag.

"My father says that, when one of my songs is on the radio or television, the dog sits by with his ears pricked up. He knows it's me."

"Ladies and Gentlemen", the album is obviously offered as a tongue-in-cheek reminder to the events in Los Angeles. My people thought the event may have been stage-managed as a publicity stunt with the album. George is adamant. "I wish I'd thought of it!" he laughs.

Ken Morley

If you'd asked Ken Morley about his life and career two decades ago the answer would have been completely different from what it is today. We know him as one of the best character actors, from amiable bunglers such as the SS Commander in 'Allo, 'Allo to the monstrous Reg Holdsworth in Coronation Street. He started his career as a teacher, as many comics do, there seems to be a natural connection between education and comedy! "I was so down on my luck at one stage that I returned to teaching. But you don't get anywhere if you don't try. My chance came when a director called offering me a big part in a TV commercial. I resigned my teaching job on the spot and set off for London.

"If ever I am inclined to get a bit pompous or self-important I think back to those heady days. Well you'll remember the TV chimps in the PG Tips adverts. Always remember that before you see any action from a chimp there has to be an actor testing for camera angle and such like. Yes, you've guessed! That was my big chance! I was a chimp's stand in!

"They do say never work with children or animals, I know why – they end up on the television and you don't. It's as simple as that."

Home for him is the Lancashire village close to where he was born in Whittle-Le-Woods, shared with the family of wife and son, and his two dogs Humphrey and Bruin, Lancashire Heelers.

Heelers have been part of his life for quite a time. He remembers chasing the charabancs down the street on their way to Blackpool and "the lights" with a Heeler at his heels. They are cross of Terrier and Corgi and, as you might imagine, have a determined streak a mile wide. They date back to the time when seventeenth century Welsh farmers walked their sheep to the markets of Manchester and were bred to keep the animals in line by nipping their heels.

One of his Granddad's Heelers saved the young Ken's life. Granddad was determined that Ken would continue the family calling — farming — and put Ken up on the

high horse and cart and gave him the reins. "The horse shot off like lightening with me clinging for dear life. Buzzer one of the Heelers gave chase and nipped at the horse's heels barking and snapping. Mum was furious with my granddad but Buzzer and I were always great pals after that. I feel a sort of affinity for the breed and my family wouldn't be complete without them.

"You don't get a chance to be lazy when you've Heelers. They love nothing better than a good long walk in the not too distant hills of Rivington. There's a peace on those hills that's a million miles from the cares of the busy world and I just thank God for the joys of the day."

Fiona Phillips

A face we all know from the couch beside Eamonn Holmes on GMTV is Fiona Phillips. Part of the support system for her hardworking journalist life comes from her dog Bismark. "We mostly call him Bizzy or Biz for short and the name suits him very well. He is a Weimaraner who is absolutely gorgeous. I've had him since he was six weeks old. I wanted a dog called Mozart because of the German Connection but Bizzy does suit him better."

What made her choose such an unusual dog? "I remember seeing one on the beach at Tenby in Wales when I was a very little girl. He matched the colour of the sand and he was just so gorgeous that I have always wanted one. They look very noble and are so intelligent. Does she think we choose a pet that resembles us in some way? "Um – nor really! I love dogs with short coats so that you can see the lines of their beautiful muscular bodies. I don't think my body exactly matches that!"

But Bismark is not Fiona's first dog. The accolade goes to a Beagle called Rufus who does sound a bit of a handful. "Rufus was my first dog when we lived in Brighton. My brother David and I had always wanted a dog and Dad wanted one too, but both my parents worked and thought it would be irresponsible to have a dog and leave alone all day and that's what I think too.

him with my parents for a while because six months in quarantine would have been too much for him. Mum and Dad seem to have fallen in love with him so I am beginning to wonder if my plan to bring Bizzy back to London will ever work out!"

But dogs were not Fiona's first experience of pet ownership. From the age of about four, she had a series of goldfish, the first was called Emma, but none of them seemed to last very long. "I think it is really important for children to have pets because when a pet dies it is the first really important jolt into the real world. I was inconsolable when my first goldfish died, and each one was remembered properly with a ceremony in the back garden. The death of Emma the first goldfish was the hardest to take. After that it seemed to become easier. It was good for me. Everything else went rosily unless I was being told off for something I'd done!"

What other pets would she have given the chance? "I would like to have a country house and keep sheep, cows and a donkey. I've always loved donkeys. They have wonderful eyes and such an appealing downtrodden look about them."

Circumstances changed and we acquired Rufus who was very, very naughty. He had that hunting instinct in him and we couldn't keep him in! If the door was open he'd be out of the door and off. He was always running away! Everybody knew him and would say 'Your Rufus was round this morning'. We moved to Southampton and lived in a house with a high fence and really tried to keep him in. He still got out this time - he dug a hole under the fence! He used to meet me from school and really embarrass me by standing and barking outside the classroom! He was a real character. But the most devastating experience came from Rufus. My mother had my youngest brother when I was about 12 and Rufus became rather vicious. I don't know whether he was getting overprotective, we tried to give him away to a farmer but it didn't work out.

"My first real experience of dogs comes from Bismark though. He spends a lot of time with my parents when I'm away. He doesn't like kennels. When he comes out he has scratches all over his nose where he has tried to dig his way out. He is such a needy dog. He always seems to need human company. When I went to the States working I thought I would be able to take him with me but eventually I realised that it would be better to leave

Sir Cliff Richard

When it comes to pets, there is one breed that is top of the charts for pop legend Sir Cliff Richard – the West Highland Terrier. Sir Cliff currently owns two Westies, Misty and Amy, and finds them a constant source of enjoyment. What was it about the Westie that made them just right for you? "I read a lot about them and one of the things that appealed to me is t hat they can entertain themselves," he says. "You can leave them in the garden and there is no need to worry about them. They are tough l ittle creatures yet so affectionate."

Due to his hectic lifestyle, Sir Cliff is in constant demand around the world, whether giving concerts or starring in the stage musical Heathcliffe.

As a result he often has to leave Amy and Misty (pedigree name Mistletoe Missy) behind, but fortunately he has a very willing dog-sitter on hand. "The lady who cleans for us just loves to have them," he says. "She lives near us in Weybridge and I can just give her a ring and drop them off. They don't even say goodbye, they enjoy being with her so much. They don't pine or anything but when they do see us again, they go absolutely wild.

"I think it's really good that we can leave them with friends.

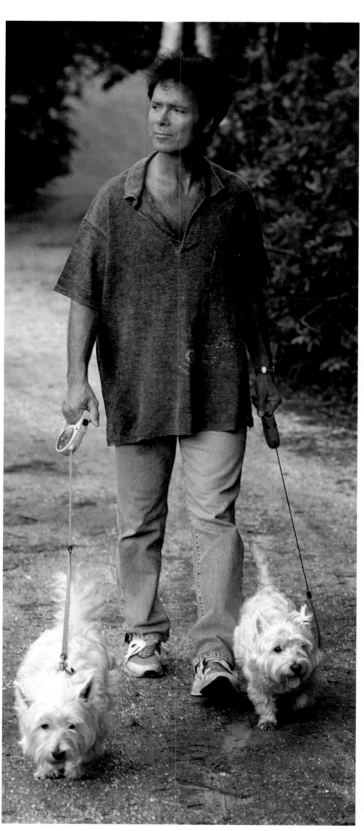

They have never been kenneled and I don't think we ever will. When we leave them we know that they are not going to be a pain and start chewing up rugs trying to get back to us."

It's been a very well-kept secret that Sir Cliff has dogs. And he explains that Misty and Any are not the first Westies he has owned. His first of the breed was called Emma but before that he had Kelly who was a Labrador cross.

"Kelly was one of my favourite dogs," he recalls. "She was 14 when she died. The vet said that she had had a great life and that it was time for us to let her go."

Sir Cliff explained why he was so fond of Kelly. "She had a strange habit that she would bark like mad when strangers came round but they soon knew that she wasn't dangerous as she would only ever bark if she had a ball in her mouth. She always carried it round with her and refused to let go of it."

Talking to Sir Cliff about his pets, both past and present, it soon becomes clear that he is someone who cares very deeply for animals, dogs in particular.

"Amy, the older one, won't beg for a chocolate," he says. "It took her about a year before she would even give us her paw. I think she knew too that all she had to do was to look dopey and she would get a chocolate anyway. Misty on the other had, sits up and begs straight away. She even saluted for the Queen.

"I firmly believe that an animal will not do anything that it doesn't want to do," he says "and if they enjoy it and it gives

us pleasure to them that's great fun. It's also a way for us to communicate with our pets which is very important."

"I can't relate to people who can be cruel to dogs, although it may be a generalisation, they can be cruel human beings as well. How they can be cruel to creatures which can't do anything back to them I just don't understand." He went on to emphasise the point. "I don't think it's asking too much to treat animals kindly."

In his long and illustrious career Sir Cliff Richard had largely followed the old showbiz adage that it is not wise to work with animals or children and he admits that he has managed to avoid both, that he can remember! Apart from Tiny the elephant that is. Sir Cliff met

Tiny on a film set many, many years ago and he has clearly stayed with him ever after.

"There was never any problem apart from on a couple of occasions when Tiny decided to go to the toilet and she would always do it just before we were due to follow her on to the stage, " he laughs, "the smell was awful."

In spite of his busy schedule, Sir Cliff still finds plenty of time to enjoy being with his pets and he talks with evident affection about their little tricks, and he is obviously "into" the reward training methods, chocolate features quite strongly.

Wendy Richard

I always hope that Wendy Richard's life is not remotely as incident prone as that of Pauline Fowler in Albert Square. An HIV-positive son, another who has tearaway tendencies, her Arthur dead after an undeserved prison sentence. Hardly enviable!

But the last generation of viewers remember a quieter Wendy Richard. They remember her starring with John Inman and Molly Sugden in "Are you Being Served"? as Miss Shirley Brahms, and the formality of that old-fashioned servility was always endearing. Miss Brahms was known to millions in the 70s as someone who liked a good gossip and wasn't real kean about work.

But, back in Albert Square, as Pauline Fowler, Wendy Richard is now better known as the queen of soaps suds. She started in EastEnders all those years ago as the young apprentice helping out the deadly gossip Dot Cotton in the Launderette. But if she had her way, there would be a rival to Wellard and Freda on the square. There'd be a new star, Shirley Brahms, her own Cairn Terrier!

Wendy known to millions of regular viewers as long suffering Pauline Fowler would love to be able to taker her pet on to the set and see her play a major role in Britain's most watched soap.

"I'm trying to work Shirley into the show", laughs Wendy. "I think she would be sensational."

"Todd Carty, who plays my son Mark, and I have already written the script. He would find this little dog, all wet and bedraggled wandering around the square and bring it home. At first, Pauline doesn't take to it, but then all of a sudden she does, and there you have it Shirley in Albert Square."

Shirley is the first Cairn that Wendy has owned, but she is now a devoted fan of the breed.

"Certainly Shirley rules my house and that's it. She looks upon me as the merry idiot, she'll see me coming and know that she can get away with murder!"

Although she laughs and jokes about the joy that Shirley brings into her life, Wendy is very conscious of the responsibility involved in making a dog part of the family. She emphasises that there are certain things that are important when owning a dog, from both the dog's point of view and your own.

"I personally always clean up after my dog. I am very hot on that and just wish that other dog owners would do the same."

"When Shirley was about ten weeks old we had a microchip put in her neck which is the most responsible way of dog registering. Again, I think more people should take note of it."

Although she loves the breed Wendy currently just has the one Cairn, but that could all change.

"I am looking for a puppy as a companion for Shirley and I would call it Betty Slocombe. Then I would have Mrs Slocombe and Miss Brahms which would be rather good, wouldn't it?"

"When I told Molly Sugden who played Mrs Slocombe in the series she was delighted!"

Since then, Wendy has become involved with the Greyhound Trust because of the ex-racer on EastEnders.

"I think they are absolutely brilliant," she says, "they are little dogs with a wonderful nature and are very good with children."

As a responsible dog owner, Wendy is very keen to stress that choosing is the most important part. Some people choose a dog for its looks without giving too much thought to temperament.

There are many ways to make a mistake and only a few perfect breeds for your family circumstances. Among other aspects, you do have to think long and hard abut the children of the family. Even if you don't have children yourself, there will always be visitors to the house and dogs can be a real magnet for children in the park and

around town. You need them to be predictable and sound.

"I think it is a very important point for anyone thinking about owning a dog. You have got to know that your dog is safe with children."

So, does Wendy believe that a Cairn is an ideal family pet?

"I'm biased aren't I?" she laughs.

Bill Roache

For 40 years, Coronation Street has been the nation's favourite soap. And William Roache, better known as Bill, the man behind Ken Barlow, the man behind Deirdre, dizziest of the host of fascinating women, has been blotting his copybook recently by actually decking Mike Baldwin! The nation was shocked and appalled at the antics of this pillar of society, schoolteacher and longest serving character in the street. He's been there for an astounding 3900 episodes!

His first encounter with a Corrie pet was Minnie Caldwell's cat in the snug of the Rover's Return. Since then there have been Jack Duckworth's birds and Stan Odgen's famous Greyhound. He was the first to welcome Pep, the Coronation Street Dog and a Border Collie, on the set and awarded him a rubber bone as a present

He has a fair collection of his own animals, particularly cats, which he admits are his favourites. He has three cats now. As a child he remembers his favourite cat. "Pru was my childhood pal, a huge Tabby who used to sleep in the black kitchen grate of our fire range. If you disturbed her she would open her mysterious eyes really wide and purr displeasure in that certain tone that only cats have I used to feed her my breakfast kippers. Mother thought I loved them. I wasn't too sure, but Pru certainly did."

He thinks that it's a good idea for children to have access to pets so they can learn the respect of all animals. "Some children do not know what a dog or cat actually is and they're frightened of it."

He also remembers a lovely Welsh Collie called Patch who lived to a great age. He remembers that she was a bit on the plump side for a Welsh Collie so she may not have been pure-bred. Childhood is obviously a warm memory for Bill.

He remembers his academic career as unspectacular though he was expected to follow his father and grandfather into medicine, but instead won prizes for acting. Bill's mother was an amateur actress who specialised in the "Murder in the Red Barn" and "Maria Martin" type of melodrama left over from the Victorian theatre. Never sure if it was for real or not, Bill remembers urging his father to rescue her as he watched the evil moustache-twirling baddie attempting to run off with his mother. She topped up her acting prowess with a fine singing

voice and often took the lead soprano part in Gilbert and Sullivan, "The White Horse Inn" and "The Desert Song".

Bill followed her lead in his two years of National Service where, as a captain in one of the British Army's remotest outposts, he adopted a desert rat as a pet.

"I happened upon a group of Arabs who were preparing for dinner. I noticed a Jerboa rat and realised that this was dinner! They are a bit hamster-like, Jabby was swapped for a tin of British bully beef and was mad a decent home in an old ammo box, happy as a sand rat! Until he was discovered by a desert owl, who ate him!"

Then he found a wounded owl and nursed it back to health with enormous patience and care. Unfortunately it was a tasty snack for a passing desert fox. Bill seems to be supporting his own food chain, and sure enough the desert fox tired to eat Bill's nose. He still bears the scar!

When he left the services he bequeathed the fox to his sergeant and his new owner's care was also rewarded by a pretty nasty nip. Sadly, the fox did not survive this insubordination and was shot.

He remembers with affection that his first leading role was at the front end of a pantomime horse! He had started the pantomime season by playing one of the ugly sisters in Cinderella but it all went horribly wrong when his make-up started to melt under the stage lights. His complaints led

to an even hotter part as the horse!

The security that Coronation Street has offered has enabled Bill to devote a lot of his energy to his pets. He has six dogs, lots of cats and cares for 15 horses. Five of the horses are his own.

"We often go over the hills round the Manchester area with our five dogs. There's Abigail, who is my favourite – she follows me everywhere. But she does tend to be jealous if she sees us stroke anyone else's dog. And there's Winston, Ella, Claude and Toby, all Labradors, and 'Orrible' Enry the Miniature Dachshund who is a bit of a handful, nippy and nasty, until he sits on your lap, then he's happy. But he's bitten all of us over the years."

There's also Charlie the cat to keep order in the household. There are three cats in all but he has to admit that Charlie is his favourite, his black and white beauty. "They all come for walks with us, and we gather all the other local cats too – it's quite a sight!

"Our whole lives seem to revolve around the animals and they are such characters. No sooner do I open the door than the Labradors are jumping up. 'Orrible' Enry is snapping at my heels and Charlie has pinched the best chair."

Bill presents the perfect picture, though, of a contented man, at peace with himself. But keep an eye on Ken Barlow, things are far from smooth.

Gaby Roslin

To be truly mad about Dogs you really have to start young. Gaby Roslin, new presenter for BBC1's coverage of Cruft's, co-presenter of Children in Need, and much more besides.

Gaby is from London, and started her acting career really young. But her first job was presenting on Cable Superchannel, then moving on to present the children's show 'Hippo'. Next came 'Motormouth', another children's Saturday morning show during the spring of 1992. Spring 1992 was the big breakthrough, with the Big Breakfast , as co-presenter with Chris Evans which did neither of them any harm in their careers. It was also a big time for Channel 4, their first big success, beating the BBC into a cocked hat. And even drawing level with GMTV! Quite an achievement.

'The Real Holiday Show' has been a more recent success, with its offshoots, 'The Real Wedding Show' and 'The Real Christmas Show' also doing well. And by now, with success in the bag, Gaby decided that what she was missing was a dog. So a dear dog called Chester became part of her life.

She grew up with a Staffordshire Bull Terrier called Bazooka. "Then I strayed a bit and in time I think I had a couple of guinea pigs and a few rabbits and we had two water tortoises – not terrapins - they were big water tortoises. One of them only died a couple of years ago, he was the same age as me!" But it usually happens that people who have dogs don't last long without them.

"After the Staffi died we got a standard long-haired Dachshund and when she had puppies and we kept one. After the Dachs, Dad had a couple of Basset Hounds."

To Gaby a house isn't a home without a dog in it. So after long discussions and deliberations with her husband Chris, she chose Chester a charming Cavalier King Charles Spaniel, to be the apple of her eye, although as the story unfolds it is fairer to say that he chose her.

From a Staffi to a Cavalier is, to any one's mind, a bit of a large jump. Even Dachshund to Cavalier is quite a step. What was it about a Cavalier that stole her heart after the assortment of dogs she remembers from childhood? And why Chester in particular? It sounds like one of those happy accidents.

"Well, Chester found me more than I found him. My boyfriend and I had long discussions about it. Then I just couldn't wait any longer. One day when I was doing the Big Breakfast. I went to a place that was recommended to me to look at a litter of pups. I saw this cute little one and picked him up. I said to him, 'Hello Chester'. As I walked away, he followed me and that was it. He didn't leave my side. I really

surprised my boyfriend, when I went to pick him up at the airport, there was the dog sitting on my lap!"

Chester obviously misses Gaby when she is working. "Oh no, I don't think so! He watches me on the television and always used to get up especially early for the Big Breakfast, but really he's an EastEnders Dog through and through. He also loves the late night films, even afternoon films when I used to fall asleep. He always stuck with it to the bitter end!

I sometimes wished he could have told me what happened!"

Gaby carefully hasn't mentioned what he does when he sees any animals on the television. Does he bother with them? "He's a scream when he's watching animals on television, he barks at anything with four legs and copies what they do!"

He sounds like a serious case of a telly addict! "If you're watching the television and you put your hand in front of his eyes, he puts his paw up to try to move it out of the way because he wants to watch the telly!"

And he seems to be fairly choosy about what he watches? "Oh, he certainly is! He also turns the channel over on the remote control. We haven't trained him to do it, it's just funny when he does it. He loves to show off and sort of rolls over – and loves doing tricks – we've

never taught him. He's a very, very clever dog. We can never get over him. The amazing thing about him is the people who are phobic or slightly frightened of dogs who come up to him and get over their fear with Chester which is great."

They say that birds of a feather flock together. Chester apparently found you, so does Gaby think he might resemble her in some way? "Well yes, we looked at certain dogs we wanted – we knew we needed a small dog. We didn't want a big dog that needed a lot of exercise – because we have such bizarre timetables, and funnily enough he is like us. I suppose he's full of life and loves television."

It all sounds as though he might be a bit of a contrast with the Staffi?

"Oh, Bazooka was great, he used to be full of energy. He'd run up and down the hall like a lunatic – he was so fantastic with kids and he used to sit with us - I mean I was too young to remember – but apparently he used to burrow in our prams and cots, and whenever the babies were having their afternoon sleep he used to make sure that everything was all right.

"But I admit I was tempted by a Labrador, and I was really taken by the

idea of Pippin, a real old-fashioned cheeky chappie mongrel, like the NCDL have as their mascot dog, the little black and white dog."

Dog ownership seems to be out of fashion a t t h e

moment. The number of dogs in this country has gone down by about two million fairly recently. Does Gaby think

it's because people are settling down later and don't want the responsibility of dogs?

"Possibly, and when they have kids they don't want a dog – so maybe everything's happening later. It's not a cheap alternative, owning a dog. I always get terribly upset when I hear about all the strays. I went and visited a Blue Cross rescue centre recently, and I get terribly upset when I see the way people treat animals."

Gaby is clearly deeply affected by the way that people treat their animals and from her point of view when we choose a dog, we are

It's a long way from impromptu stand-up spots at the Vauxhall Tavern to being made custodian of the most famous cheque book and pen in the business but Lily Savage has taken it all in her stiletto-shod stride.

With a wit as dry as the desert and mass of hair set like a giant blonde meringue Lily's sharply observed views on life have made her a major star. From fronting the Big Breakfast for a year to her own show and now as the new host of Blankety Blank, Lily is one of TV's most famous faces. But what lies behind that chirpy scouse façade? Would the real Lily Savage please stand up…

Although the idea was an interview with Lily, the reality turned out to be a far more interesting experience.

The address was an apartment near to Tower Bridge. The door was opened by a tall, good-looking former ship's cook and there wasn't a trace of diamante or mascara in sight.

Paul O'Grady is the man behind Lily Savage and like his famous alter ego, he's witty, charming and great fun to be with.

He shares his home in the capital with one of the cutest bundles of fur you're ever likely to see. Buster is part Bichon Frise and part Shih Tzu and has almost as many fans as Lily herself.

"He's a real oddball," says Paul of the small white fluffball that

Lily Savage

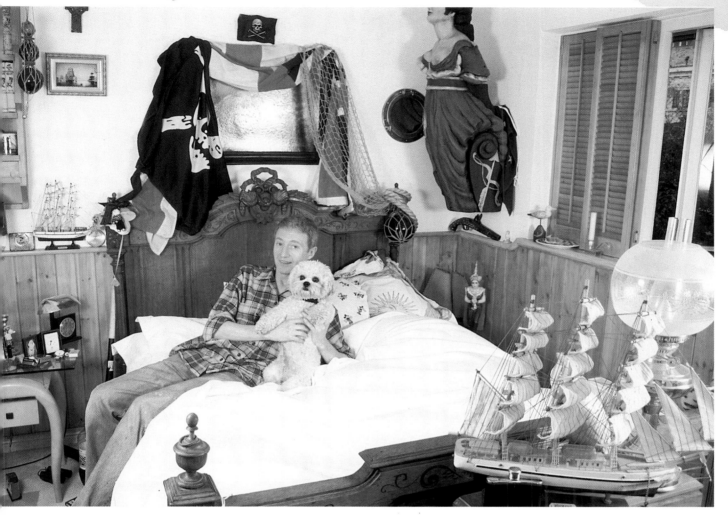

learly believes that licking is a great way to say hello. "He turned up one morning near Christmas at the Big Breakfast studio and I ended up taking him home."

Buster is a real showbiz luvvie. He's been on TV since he was 10 weeks old and he loves the stage," adds Paul.

He sits in the wings and watches me and sometimes he'll come on during the act."

When Paul and Buster set out for a walk from their recently acquired home its always Buster

not Paul who draws the crowds. Out of character, no one recognises Paul as one of TV's hottest properties, but Buster always proves a big hit, particularly with the tourists around Tower Bridge.

Away from his fans, Buster is clearly settled with Paul in London. In one corner of the living room you'll find over 30 different dog toys, all sent in by fans who had seen Buster on the Big Breakfast.

"Every day he selects one to play with" says Paul. "He takes them all out of the box and

looks at them, then takes one to his cushion in the middle of the room, then puts all the other back. He never has more than one toy at a time on the cushion and that's his for the day".

So much for Buster, but what about Queenie who Lily often refers to on stage and in TV shows. Well - the truth is that Queenie the whippet doesn't actually exist. She is in reality Lily's fictional pet and as far as Paul's concerned Buster is all the canine companionship he needs.

Now 42, Paul O'Grady is clearly very content with sharing his life with "that woman" as he describes Lily.

However, Superstar she may be but it is clear that she does not dominate his life.

The home betrays Paul's love of the sea, a legacy of his childhood in Birkenhead.

"That doesn't mean we were posh," he laughs. "We lived in Tranmere. The tunnel came out and there was our house Cammell-Laird's ship yards and the abattoir!

After leaving the sea behind Paul moved to London and performed as part of a drag trio around the pubs and clubs of the capital before Lily established herself as the compere at the Vauxhall pub.

From there fame and fortune were just around the corner including TV appearances and a recent 32-week tour in Prisoner Cell Block H.

The Lily Savage Show currently being screened by the BBC is just the latest spell in the limelight with that great family favourite Blankety Blank now firmly on our TV schedules.

But whatever happens to Lily, Paul makes sure that Buster is never too far away.

"I pack my bag and Buster goes and puts his lead and bowl in. He knows what's going on," says Paul.

There are many advantages of being a pocket–sized pooch including the ability to be smuggled into hotels that don't accept dogs.

"I'll put him in a bag and he never says a word. Mind you once we're in the room he gives the game away by growling but we've never been asked to leave."

But be honest when you're one of TVs hottest properties – and a really nice person to boot who is ever going to ask you to leave!?

"But the view was fantastic, my bedroom looked out across the Mersey and all my family had been merchant sailors. There were lots of ships then and I miss it now. I'd like a view over the Thames, but the prices!"

Paul went to sea as a teenager –

to the Philippines as a ship's cook – and his home reflects this love of things nautical. The staircases look like ship's companionways with cleverly concealed lighting giving the impression of being aboard a ship at night; the walls are adorned with shipping posters.

Chris Tarrant

"Who wants to be a Millionaire" as before is winning the television ratings war. It's hard to remember quiz shows before Chris Tarrant! Chris Tarrant as question master extraordinare makes a lovely job of host, he's warm and cheerful, sympathetic to a fault when it all goes wrong, and is brilliant at putting people at their ease in a studio setting.

The new series is justly popular and is breaking with tradition in its format, but is so popular that its producers say it is watched by people who normally have no time for quiz shows. It is appealing because it puts real people in a dramatic setting, and is doubly appealing in that we know in advance what each person is planning to do with the million. Miss it and you know that Mrs Jones of Sudbury won't get that luxury cruise or Mr Fletcher of Lyme Regis will have to make do with another ten years of prehistoric potting shed! The series has evolved, but the seeds of greatness were there from the beginning. Chris Tarrant was their first and only choice as host.

Chris was brought up with a wide assortment of pets, "numerous rabbits, hundreds of goldfish, all colours, shapes and sizes of budgies and a hamster that I thought had gone into hibernation two weeks after I bought it – but I found that it had died!"

out of our cars where she will happily sleep for hours on end. She does come fishing with me at the weekends — which she does seem to enjoy."

"She really loves going fishing and when we get near our favourite place — about two miles away — she starts wimpering from the back of the car and going round in circles getting more and more excited."

Labradors are a very popular breed with families, is this why he chose her or was he tempted to have a dog that was a little more unusual?

"We went for a Labrador mainly because we knew they were very safe with children, very much a family dog and they are a decent size. I have no time for little yappy dogs at all."

"If I had to describe Bimbo's character in three words it would have to be lovable, loyal and daft. We tried to train her. My wife Ingrid took her to obedience classes but she has become justly famous as a bit of an escapologist, quite a community character and I think the locals feed her every morning.

"She's quite a comedian as well. I remember one particular incident where she got trapped in a dustbin. We chased her round for ages to try to get it off but we couldn't catch her!

"More recently she ran off with someone's Sunday joint. She arrived home with a large leg of lamb — ready cooked — in her mouth!"

But there were no dogs in the Tarrant household at the time, "because we lived in a busy part of Reading and it wouldn't have been a good place for the dog to roam free".

We had Bimbo as a pup about seven years ago and none of us had ever had a dog before. The children had had rabbits and chinchillas, none of which lasted very long. We chose Bimbo because we thought she would be a friend and a protector for the children.

"She is most at home in the Warwickshire house, where she roams round the fields with all of us, chasing the rabbits, sniffing out foxes and badger holes.

"During the week where we live in Esher Surrey while I do my Capital Radio show every morning, it's more difficult to take her out and about, but she spends her time leaping in and

the most cramped and filthy conditions. Thankfully most of these are now being closed down."

The advice from old pros in the acting profession is that working with children and animals is dangerous because they tend to upstage you. Has he ever worked with animals on television? Chris's experiences sound rather more dramatic and dangerous. "I need danger money! Over the years I've worked with a real variety of animals, usually quite disastrously. There was a flying chimp in Nashville who landed me a black eye, a boxing kangaroo that gave me a good kicking, and an elephant that dropped its shoulders with me on its back and threw me a very long way. All the way on live television naturally!"

With four children, the cats and the rest of the menagerie it would be fairly natural to liken the Tarrant home life to a zoo! But what does he think about zoos?

"I have no problem with the larger zoos or safari parks, where the animals are genuinely cared for and in some cases, have probably been saved from virtual wipe out in the wild. But I hate the very small zoos that I've seen around the world where the poor animals are kept in

As the pigeon fancying, pint pulling Jack Duckworth, actor Bill Tarmey has spent many hours on our TV screens working with animals.

During his time on the nation's favourite soap, he has become a role model for pigeon lovers around the country - often preferring the company of his feathered friends to that of 'er indoors, the formidable Vera.

He has also been the would-be greyhound trainer and is currently harboring hopes of striding into the winner's enclosure as part-owner of the racehorse Betty's Hotshot.

"People sometimes think I really am Jack Duckworth", says Bill. "The old dears stop me in the supermarket and tell me where the bird food is. Someone even sent a copy of a pigeon fanciers newspaper to Granada addressed to Mr Duckworth."

Away from the Street, Bill Tarmey is just as fond of animals as his larger than life character appears to be.

At his home outside Manchester, Saatchi a large Doberman cross and a cat named Sam are very much part of the family.

Indeed Sam is very much in charge of the Tarmey household, often to be seen wandering around with the air of a true Aristocat.

Bill is fond of recounting tales of Sam's nocturnal wanderings which have, on occasions caused no little chaos.

Bill Tarmey

He recalls: "We had friends to stay over for the weekend and forgot to introduce them to the cat, which was a mistake.

"Later that night we heard this almighty scream. Sam had entered the guest room via the window and landed on top of the bed. I don't know what they thought it was but the screaming lasted quite a while.

"Next morning the atmosphere was rather strained to say the least until Sam waltzed in blissfully unaware of the mayhem he had created. As soon as my mate's wife clapped eyes on the cat she realised what had landed on her in the midnight hour, though I'm still not certain they could see the funny side of it".

For as long as he can remember Bill Tarmey has always had a pet dog to keep him company – Saatchi being the latest in a long line of canine companions.

Bill believes that owning a pet, particularly a dog, brings something very special to the

household. His children have grown up learning to respect and understand the needs of their animal friends.

"It's the finest way of teaching a child to accept responsibility I know", says Bill. "You get a tiny puppy that has joined your family with all its trust and hope – you can see it in the little thing's eyes – then together you develop a relationship.

"That is a wonderful thing. It brings meaning and love to the home as the kids begin to recognise that this puppy's life depends on them. What better way can there be for a child to understand the nature of trust and compassion for God's creatures."

Not every pet Bill has owned has shown him the same level of understanding however.

He has particularly fond memories of Django, the Manchester Terrier, whom he owned while still a club singer.

"The Group did all the latest hits and I always practised them in the front room. Django used to sit on the couch and listen with his ears up and head on one side. I could tell if he didn't like a song as he'd dash upstairs and hide under the bed."

Although a central character in Coronation Street for many years, the young Bill Tarmey turned his hand to almost everything including Shakespeare.

He even worked with the great Sir Laurence Olivier where he was supposed to ride up to the great man, dressed in full

Medieval armour. And then deliver his line.

Bill remembers the experience well. "I'd never been on anything bigger than a Blackpool Donkey," he says, "and this horse was more like Blackpool Tower.

"It stood at least 17 hands and probably weighed half a ton. I was kitted out in armour, carrying a sword and just climbing on was a feat of daring.

"It was all I could do to stay in the saddle. Then some kind soul assisted by slapping it on the buttocks and off we lurched in

the Sir Laurence's direction. We failed to stop and I ended up shouting my line over my shoulder much to his amusement."

Although he may have literally been taken for a ride on this occasion, Bill firmly believes in the value of being an animal lover.

"If at all possible introduce a pet into your life. The love and affection you give them will be returned in abundance. You just can't be lonely with a pet, they won't let you. One wag of your pal's tail and where are the cares? All gone."

Anthea Turner gives the impression that she is a contented soul, and that seems to be close to the truth.

"I am a really optimistic person most of my time though I do have my moments. I tend to be happiest doing what I am doing. I always seem to muddle through. I have been really fortunate with what I have achieved and it has all really been a happy accident.

"I was at a party way back in 1986, at the time I was working in PR for a radio station, and someone asked me if I knew anyone who might fancy having a go at video jockeying a music show for Sky TV. Funnily enough I did, and it was me!"

Would she say she had role models and who are they?

"When I was little, I thought Olivia Newton-John was the height of style. I dressed like her and looked a bit like her too, I thought."

And the career highlight?

"It was a fantastic time on Blue Peter. I am quite adventurous and the opportunities that came my way were fantastic. I know that you can get stuck and typecast working on children's television but that isn't why I left. There are many more opportunities now that there are more stations, and I think that women can have an easier time than men. The business has changed a lot, is much more cut-throat than it used to be.

"I was offered the job of a lifetime on GMTV and couldn't say no. But if I hadn't been offered that job I am quite happy to say that I would be on Blue Peter still!

"It was on Blue Peter that I first met Golden Retrievers, dear old Bonnie!, and at the time I was determined that as soon as I was able I would have one of my own. Grant said that one Retriever just wasn't enough. And he was quite right. We have two and they get on so well together, just rolling around and playfighting together that it wasn't double trouble as I had assumed.

"We always had an assortment of cats, dogs, gerbils, at home when we were growing up and I always said that as soon as I could I would have a houseful. Now I have six horses, three cats – all black – Oliver, Olive and Twiglet two of them lived with me in London, but apart from them all the others have arrived in the last year since I have been living in the country with my boyfriend. Budie and Digger are the dogs, both Golden Retrievers. They are about a year old and full of fun and always playing and rolling around, just like the cats. I have a Horse that I bought in Malaga, a real grey beauty from Andalusia. I had always wanted a stallion with full Spanish blood. He is absolutely gorgeous, as good as gold and stands about 15.3 hands. Johnny Rebel is Grant's, my boyfriend's, a really big horse, who stands 17 hands.

The cats and dogs, and all the pets get on really well. "All of my cats are rescue cats. Oliver is Wendy's really but her husband Gary is allergic to him, so he came to live with me, and like cats do, he made himself instantly at home. The three cats get on famously. The boys just play all day but Olive is a bit stand-offish. Obviously ill treatment worries me.

"It worries me that people buy a pet and then start to think about its needs. It seems that some people get dogs that are perhaps unsuited to their lifestyle, they might be too big or need more exercise than people have time for. I know that dogs need company and lots of space to run around in.

"Dogs for the disabled is a charity that is very close to my heart. I first heard about them through Blue Peter during 1993 where we covered a story about a young woman called Ann Greenwood whose life was changed through her dog. Funnily enough the dog was called Shep! I can remember the marvelous things that dog could do.

"I stayed in contact with the charity and in my next animal-orientated programme, Pet Power, I came across another chap with MS who also said how much he had been helped by having a dog through Dogs for Disabled. Most people think that the charity is just another version of Guide Dogs for the Blind, but a dog for Dogs for Disabled has to be much more versatile. There is far more to a Dogs for the Disabled dog than just a guiding machine. The dog is a

companion and friend, as well as helper and security system.

"I first became actively involved at the Liverpool Victoria Snooker Tournament in 1998 where I was hosting the event. The chosen charity was Dogs for the Disabled and Steve Davis, as their champion for the day awarded all his winnings directly to Dogs for Disabled. I had the chance to renew my acquaintance with the work of the charity and some of the clients that day. Dogs for Disabled's 150th dog was named Snooks after the event and her training was supported directly by the prize money donated that day. I think we made about £14,000. I was asked if I would like to become Vice Patron of the Charity and I was absolutely delighted to accept."

Natalie Barnes has had quite a year! The Rover's Return is never quite as inviting when she isn't behind the bar but now she's as regular there as she can be. Sometimes, The Street's siren is so busy pulling men she's hardly time to pull the pints.

Denise Welch is the actress behind Natalie. She loves doing Coronation Street "because it keeps me close to home and my family. It's literally a 30-minute drive to work. I'm very lucky".

Like many actresses Denise has made the transition from stage to screen effortlessly. "I prefer television now," she says, "but when I'm doing theatre I prefer that."

Her proudest moments? "It is difficult to choose but I think the high point in my career was seeing 'Soldier, Soldier' for the first time. The quality of the series was fantastic – good writing, and though I say it myself, it was a very rewarding part for me.

"But the real proud moments are when my family are all there to see me, that's a real thrill."

Denise has certainly had a busy time of it. Her theatre credits include a rare variety from 'Grease' at the Leicester Haymarket, to a national tour of 'There's a girl in my soup'.

Her face is perhaps better known from her television triumphs including not only

Denise Welch

'Soldier, Soldier', but 'Byker Grove' and 'Spender' as well as sharing the limelight with Tim for "Auf Wiedersehen Pet".

She plays a cat-lover – Tiger is her cat - in "The Street" but it's Sadie the Boxer that steals the show at home.

"She has made such a difference to our lives. And I can't imagine life without her". Sadie is now four years old, they acquired her at four months, the last of the litter. To complete the family, there's Tim Healey her husband and Matthew their 10 year old son.

Like many family dogs, Sadie was really bought for Matthew. "He's an only child and I think it teaches children the care of living creatures when there are pets in the house. Though he's a bit of a fair-weather dog walker. Tim does the evil days when it's really raining hard."

"Where I was brought up in Whitley Bay, my first pet was a budgie called Kettle – I really can't remember where the name came from. (Polly put the kettle on maybe?)

"My start in dogs wasn't particularly good. I had a lovely little dog called Candy when I was about eight or nine. But she disappeared one day and never came back. I was absolutely

heartbroken. After that my parents said that we wouldn't have another one – we were all devastated. But when I was 12 there was Sam the pony.

"It was a real surprise," remembers Denise. "I'd done the thing that lots of little girls do up and down the country. 'Can I have a pony? I'll never want anything for my birthday or Christmas ever again, honestly'. I got home from a day out with my friend and there was a crowd of people in the back garden. I just had to go and find out what was going on. I rode Sam at shows for about five years and then drama

school, oh, and boys took over my life!"

Dogs, though crept back into the drama student's life.

"When I went to drama college in London, someone gave my boyfriend and me a yellow Labrador puppy we called Howard. The lifestyle just didn't suit dogs so I played pathetic and asked my parents if they would care for him for a few weeks. I hoped they would be all right about it and fortunately they loved him so much that they kept him all of his long life. He only died about five years ago, and he was 14 years old."

Why did she choose a Boxer? "My granny had a

Boxer called Chester and I can remember riding on his back when I was about five. Sadie is so funny. When Tim comes home, she spends ages licking his bald head! Oh, and she walks like a crab sort of sideways. But she is not a barmy boxer, like some of them are. We have a friend who also has a Boxer which is an absolute nutcase. Fortunately Sadie is quite sedate. We are very lucky to have her."

Having two careers in one house can often mean that you have to spend long periods apart. But Denise and Tim, together for over 10 years are lucky in having lives that can mesh together without the usual professional strains. "Though for many years, throughout 'Auf Wiedersehen Pet', Tim was more famous than me. I was simply known as Tim Healey's wife. I do enjoy being recognised and I love the parties."

Denise had another birthday surprise to top the pony, when Tim whisked her away for a surprise slap-up party for her 40th last year. Family, friends and colleagues had a wild old time at a hotel in the heart of Cheshire. The wine flowed and the whole cast of Corrie had a whale of a time. We even had Brooksiders there and the Leicester City Football Team gatecrashed! The family band took over the stage at one point as son Matthew played the drums, dad Tim fronted his own Blues Band, Denise took control of the microphone and belted out the song that made "Soldier, Soldier" – "you don't have to say you love me" with Janice Battersby as backing vocalist. It was a night to remember.

Denise is keen for Matthew to understand about the responsibilities of caring for Sadie, and Denise and Tim set a good example by ensuring that she is always looked after.

"We are very lucky in that we have relations who live very close and Sadie loves them to bits. So she has never had to go into kennels in her life. "My advise to anybody thinking about getting a dog is to think carefully about it and not to get one if you are not prepared to commit 100 per cent to it. And a dog will always be the most rewarding if you treat it as part of the family".

Denise is always so busy on our screens and it is always a sheer pleasure to see her face – the more times, the merrier.

Edward Woodward

These include Barnaby, the Bernese Mountain Dog, two King Charles Spaniels, Rosy and Rags, and two ponies. It's Barnaby who both through his size and personality tends to be the focus of attention when Edward's at home.

"The dogs are not allowed to get up on the furniture. A couple of chairs are just for them. They all know that, but Barnaby, being the biggest, tries to take advantage. When Barnaby sits on an armchair you literally can't see it. When Barnaby lies on the couch, the whole couch is full of Barnaby. He's hardly unobtrusive but the thing is he thinks he is.

"He gets up on a chair and he thinks he can't be seen and he sits there and looks so surprised when you go up and say 'get off'. There's a look of total astonishment on his face as if to say 'How did you know I was here?'

"Rosy and Rags spend their whole time playing with the cats. One of the cats is totally convinced he is a dog and he certainly acts more like a dog than a cat."

Edward's love for dogs dates back to his childhood during the war. The family pet then was called Chum "a real Heinz variety of a dog", remembers Edward. "He was an absolute joy and a great friend. And he was very much a wartime dog because he had the most astonishing sixth sense and would run to the air raid shelter about four minutes before an air raid warning sounded. We all used to go down to the shelter with him and sure enough he was never wrong."

Sadly Chum suffered the fate of many wartime pets. The Woodward family home was bombed and the noise and turmoil of the bombing upset the balance of the sensitive dog's mind.

Dogs have continued to be a particular favourite for Edward. "Dogs are totally and absolutely loyal and willing to be the centre of attention and make you the centre of their life. This has been proved over and over again. Dogs have a desperate need to be loved and cared for and a desperate need at the same time to love and care for the person who owns them or the family they are with".

Throughout his career Edward has worked with animals on numerous occasions.

"I'm terrible for names and dates," he says. "But I did a film in Australia some years ago – 'Breaker Morant' – which won lots of awards and the horse I rode was absolutely marvellous. The film was about seven weeks of actual shooting and two

weeks rehearsing and I spent about five weeks on horseback.

"He was a great trained horse. You wanted it to walk and it walked, gallop it galloped and I loved doing it. In the old days they used to be very cruel to horses in Hollywood when they'd even put up wires to trip them up. It was pretty horrifying but they are not like that these days.

"I also did a film called 'Champions' and we used Aldaniti the race horse which had won the Grand National. The horse was treated far better than any of the actors. It would come out of a beautiful vehicle, then the horse was allowed to do 15-minutes work and then was allowed back into its warm dressing room and we were either in the pouring rain or in a leaking caravan.

"Although I am a lover of animals, you can get very jealous," he laughs!

In his long and illustrious career Edward Woodward regards working at the National Theatre under Lord Olivier playing 'Cyrano De Bergerac' as one of the highlights. As far as film performances, it is 'Breaker Morant' and the cult classic 'The Wicker Man' which he remembers most fondly.

To the TV loving public however 'The Equaliser' is still a favourite.

"That's still shown all over the world," he says. "I finished that four or five years ago now. I have a series in Canada, a Paramount production which is filmed in Toronto although it's supposed to be New York and is

based on a character called Harrison." With such a wide-ranging career are there any ambitions left unfulfilled?

"I'd like to do another musical", he admits, "I'd love to record ballads again. I have been offered musicals in the last five years but I haven't really been interested in any of them."

And finally, such a devoted animal lover as Edward Woodward must have a few words of advice to pet owners everywhere.

"Just love your pets," he says. "If you love them and treat them as you would want to be treated yourself then everything follows."